SCOTLAND'S STONE OF DESTINY

NICK AITCHISON

For Christina Laing, with love,
and in loving memory of James Laing (1920–2008)

First published in 2000

This paperback edition first published in 2009
Reprinted 2017

The History Press
The Mill, Brimscombe Port
Stroud, Gloucestershire, GL5 2QG
www.thehistorypress.co.uk

© Nick Aitchison, 2000, 2003, 2009

The right of Nick Aitchison to be identified as
the Author of this work has been asserted in accordance
with the Copyrights, Designs and Patents Act 1988.

All rights reserved. No part of this book may be reprinted
or reproduced or utilised in any form or by any electronic,
mechanical or other means, now known or hereafter invented,
including photocopying and recording, or in any information
storage or retrieval system, without the permission in writing
from the Publishers.
British Library Cataloguing in Publication Data.
A catalogue record for this book is available from the British Library.

ISBN 978 0 7524 5034 6

Typesetting and origination by The History Press
Printed in Great Britain by TJ International Ltd

CONTENTS

ACKNOWLEDGEMENTS

Like most Scots, I first learned about the Stone of Destiny as a child. But it was my research on early Irish royal centres that first stimulated my interest in the Stone. In 1984, Dr Stephen Driscoll kindly photocopied Archie McKerracher's article on the Stone for me and, since then, my file on the Stone has grown gradually. The announcement of the Stone's return in July 1996 prompted a flood of press comment and analysis, much of it regurgitating earlier myths and misconceptions about the Stone and its authenticity. This convinced me of the need for a wide-ranging and accessible account of the Stone in its various historical contexts. Much of the text was drafted by late 1997, but was then put aside while I completed another project. I am particularly grateful to Peter Kemmis Betty for his enthusiasm, guidance and patience, which has enabled me to see *Scotland's Stone of Destiny* to publication. I also wish to thank Anne Phipps for seeing it through the press so smoothly.

I am very grateful to many individuals and organisations who provided assistance and support during the research and writing of this book: Dr Stephen Driscoll unwittingly kindled my interest in the Stone; Dr Dauvit Broun commented on early drafts of chapters 1-4, suggesting many improvements and saving me from innumerable errors; my parents, Norma and Jim, provided an excellent press cuttings service; and the Scottish Office Information Directorate (as it was then) provided press releases and other information. I am indebted to Margaret Stewardson for the translation of the inscription recorded in Camden's *Reges, Reginae, Nobiles* and to Miss Christine Reynolds, Assistant Keeper of the Muniments in Westminster Abbey, for arranging its translation and for drawing my attention to other sources. Westminster Abbey Muniment Room and Library, the British Library Reading Room, initially at Bloomsbury and now at St Pancras, and the British Library Newspaper Library at Colindale all provided invaluable advice and facilities; I am very grateful to their staff for their patient assistance. Pat and Jon's unflagging interest in 'the book' over several years provided encouragement. But my greatest debt is to Karen for her continued patience and support.

I am also grateful to the many sources which have given permission to reproduce copyright material. Every effort has been made to trace the owners of copyright material; the author and publisher apologise to any whom it has proved impossible to trace or contact.

PREFACE

No stone ever had so wonderful a history
William Burges, in Giles Gilbert Scott, *Gleanings from Westminster Abbey* (1863)

The Stone of Destiny is unique by any standards. Few artefacts, not even the Elgin Marbles/Parthenon Frieze, have generated as much interest, controversy and passion over such a prolonged period.

The Stone, also known as the Stone of Scone and the Coronation Stone, occupies an exceptional place in British history. It is internationally famous as the sacred stone on which successive English and, after the union of the English and Scottish crowns in 1603, British monarchs have been crowned. This symbolic role stretches across the centuries from the coronation of Edward II in 1308 until, most recently, the coronation of Elizabeth II in 1953. The Stone, however, is of considerably greater antiquity than this and is at least as well known as the most ancient, emotive and enigmatic symbol of Scottish nationhood.

In a Scottish context, the Stone's significance is derived both from its symbolic function and its fate. In keeping with ancient practice, Scotland's early kings were inaugurated by being seated, not crowned, on the Stone at the ancient royal centre of Scone, near Perth. Before this, Scone was an important royal site of the Picts, an early medieval people occupying what is now north-eastern Scotland and who were absorbed by the Scots by *c*.900 to form *Alba*, the forerunner of the medieval kingdom of the Scots. The last Scottish kings to have been installed on the Stone at Scone were Alexander III, in 1249, and John Balliol, in 1292. Detailed information about their inauguration ceremonies survives. However, in 1296, during the bitter and protracted Scottish War of Independence, the Stone was seized by Edward I of England, the 'Hammer of the Scots', taken to London and installed beneath the seat of the specially-constructed Coronation Chair in Westminster Abbey. For the next 700 years, except for one brief interlude in 1950–51, when it was removed by Scottish nationalists, the Stone remained at Westminster.

The Stone's already eventful history took a dramatic turn in 1996 when the then Prime Minister, John Major, announced that the Stone was to be returned to Scotland. Amidst huge publicity on both sides of the Anglo-Scottish border, the Stone left Westminster Abbey, crossed the River Tweed into Scotland at Coldstream, and arrived with full pomp and ceremony at its new resting place in Edinburgh Castle on St Andrew's Day, 30 November 1996. The Stone's repatriation marked the end of a 700-year-long chapter of Scottish history and represented an extraordinary homecoming for one of the most famous symbols of Scottish nationhood. However, while crowds lined Edinburgh's Royal Mile to welcome the Stone back to Scotland, many Scots were either deeply sceptical or openly scornful of the significance of the Stone's restoration, the government's motives and even the Stone's authenticity. Why should an ostensibly unremarkable block of sandstone have such a long and auspicious royal past and yet still provoke popular passions and controversy?

Around the Stone's long and colourful royal history – Scottish, English and British – has accumulated an extensive body of mythology. Many of these myths are of considerable antiquity themselves, while others are more recent or are still emerging. The earliest myths focus on the Stone's origins. These relate how the Stone was either the Pharaoh's Stone or Jacob's Pillow and how it was brought from Egypt or Palestine to Scotland, via Spain and Ireland. According to mythology, the Stone was then moved from Ireland to the west coast of Scotland before arriving at Scone. More recent, but persistent and widely held, myths concern the authenticity of the Stone itself. These maintain that the Stone now in Edinburgh Castle is not just a fake – Edward I having taken the wrong stone in 1296 – but may even be a 'double fake', with the Stone removed from Westminster Abbey in 1950 having been replaced with a copy. It is on this debate that recent studies of the Stone have concentrated. Although these myths are integral to the Stone's mystique, as well as to its contemporary cultural significance, they have tended to divert attention from the Stone's wider historical importance and earlier symbolism.

The Stone's early history is obscure, masked by a thick veneer of mythology that purports to account for its origins. Indeed, there are no reliable historical references to the Stone before the inauguration of Alexander III in 1249. Myths have filled the vacuum. This book attempts to unravel the complex and sometimes emotive webs of myth and history surrounding the Stone. However, it does not attempt to chip away this concretion of myths merely to discard them. Rather, distinguishing between historical fact and fiction is an important step in exploring the significance of the Stone in its various historical and cultural contexts, as a Scottish (and perhaps originally Pictish) royal inauguration stone, English war trophy, relic of English and British royal heritage, and symbol of Scottish nationhood. A wide range of evidence is employed to elucidate these different aspects of the Stone.

Scotland's Stone of Destiny begins by considering the various names by which the Stone has been known and the prophecy from which its most widely-used name is derived. Chapter 2 looks at the myths surrounding the Stone and their function, particularly during the Scottish War of Independence, as well as the modern myths which the Stone continues to inspire. The Stone itself is examined in Chapter 3, including its appearance, features and geology. This is followed by a discussion of the Stone's possible earlier functions, concluding with a new interpretation of the Stone's original use and the source of its status as a sacred relic and symbol of Scottish kingship. The various claims concerning the Stone's disputed authenticity are reviewed in Chapter 4, concluding that the Stone installed in Edinburgh Castle in 1996 is the same as that seized by Edward I at Scone in 1296.

The Stone's association with Scone is explored in Chapter 5, beginning with the evidence for Scone's status as a major Pictish and early Scottish royal centre. This continues with the Stone's role in the inauguration of Scottish kings there, including a detailed examination of Alexander III's installation in 1249. The Stone's symbolic function is discussed with reference to accounts of similar stones and rituals elsewhere, and the cosmological symbolism of the Stone, the Moot Hill and Scone are analysed for the first time. Chapter 5 concludes with a discussion of Scone after the Stone's removal. Beginning with the Stone's seizure by Edward I in 1296, Chapter 6 covers the Stone's new symbolic role and location as the Coronation Stone upon which successive English and British monarchs have been crowned in Westminster Abbey. The myths and literary appearances which the Stone's long presence in Westminster Abbey have generated are also reviewed. Chapter 7 concerns various attempts to retrieve the Stone, from unsuccessful negotiations in the 1320s to its celebrated 'theft' from Westminster Abbey by Scottish students in 1950 and its official return to Scotland in 1996. The book concludes with an assessment of the Stone's significance in a Scotland with a renewed sense of nationhood and, for the first time since 1707, its own parliament.

AUTHOR'S NOTE

Unless otherwise stated: the Stone is the Stone of Destiny; all dates are AD; for kings, all date ranges given are regnal; for places, old (pre-1975) county names are given.

PREFACE TO THE PAPERBACK EDITION

Interest in the Stone of Destiny has continued unabated since the first publication of this book. I am very grateful to the publishers for giving me the opportunity to correct a couple of minor errors and some stylistic points in this paperback edition. Although no major revision of the text has been attempted (or, I hope, is required), I have included some additional information in support of my conclusions and added some recent publications to the bibliography.

Nick Aitchison
25 February 2003

1

THE NAME AND PROPHECY
OF THE STONE

\

> The element of uncertainty seems to enter into nearly everything that is connected
> with this stone.
>
> W.H. Stacpoole, *The Coronation Regalia* (1902)

The Stone of Destiny has been known by many names over the centuries. Now also
referred to widely as the Coronation Stone and the Stone of Scone, the uncertainty and
controversy surrounding the Stone even extends to its name. This chapter looks at the
origins and evolution of the Stone's various names, their mythological associations and
historical significance. It also considers the prophecy which is intimately associated with
the Stone and gives the Stone the name by which it is now most commonly known: the
Stone of Destiny.

MEDIEVAL AND MODERN NAMES

Whatever name or names the Stone of Destiny was referred to before it was seized by
Edward I in 1296 are probably lost. The earliest surviving sources concerning the Stone do
not predate the Stone's removal from Scone, although they may draw on earlier traditions.
The only possible exception, and probably the earliest surviving reference to the Stone, is
in the Gaelic poem *The Birth of Áedán mac Gabráin* of *c*.1060, which refers to 'the Eastern
Stone'. Over the centuries since it was taken to Westminster, the Stone has been known
by various names, ranging in popularity and longevity and providing an insight into the
Stone's changing cultural and historical significance.

The Stone's earliest recorded name, the exotic 'Pharaoh's Stone' (*lapidem Pharaonis*), appears
in *Liber Extravagans* ('Supplementary Book', or *Chronicon Rythmicum*), dating to sometime
between 1296 and 1306 (probably 1304–06). This name reflects the Stone's mythical origins:
that it was brought to Scotland from Egypt by Scota, daughter of pharaoh.

Most medieval sources, however, refer to the Stone not by name, but descriptively. One
of the earliest surviving references, in Baldred Bisset's *Processus* (1301), describes the Stone
confusingly as the 'royal seat of marble' (*sedile regiae* [i.e. *regale*] *marmorium*). This, in its
many variant forms, is how the Stone was usually referred to throughout the Middle Ages.
This attests the influence of mythology and the derivative nature of many references to the

Stone, as well as a persistent confusion between the Stone and the throne in which it may have been set. Other references to the Stone's form emphasise its perceived size. It is 'a large stone' (*una petra magna*) in Edward I's Wardrobe Accounts (royal inventories) for 1303–04.

Other medieval references to the Stone are either descriptive or by name, but tend not to be very informative. It was, in the *Life of Edward II* (*Vita Edwardi Secundi, c.*1329), simply the 'stone of famous memory' (*lapis . . . celebris memorie*), suggesting that it was so well known that it did not need a name. Several sources stress the Stone's royal associations. In both Latin and Norman French, then spoken at the English royal court, it was the 'Royal Stone': *lapidem regalem* in William of Rishanger's *Chronica et Annales* (*c.*1327), *petram regalem* in the *Life of Edward II* and *la pere real* in *Scalacronica* (1355–63). 'Royal Stone' enjoyed a revival in 1950–51, its shorter form lending itself to newspaper headlines reporting the Stone's removal from Westminster Abbey (**66**).

The Stone's Scottishness was perceived to be another defining characteristic. In several English sources it is simply the 'Stone of Scotland': *petra Scoci[a]e* in Edward I's Wardrobe Accounts for 1299–1300 and *La Piere d'Escoce* in the song of the same name (*c.*1307). The *Annals of Henry IV* combine the Stone's royal associations and its provenance: 'the stone which is called the regal stone of the kingdom of Scotland' (*lapidem, qui dicitur 'Regale regni Scotiae'*). The Stone is specifically associated with Scone: the 'kinges sette of Scone' in Langtoft's *Chronicle* and, in the *Chronicle of Lanercost* for 1327, the 'Stone of Scone' (*Lapidem de Scone*), 'upon which the Kings of Scotland used to be set at their coronation at Scone'. The Stone takes this name from the inauguration place of the Scottish kings, where it was seized by Edward I in 1296.

'Stone of Scone' is the oldest recorded and, arguably, the most historically authentic of the Stone's current names. Indeed, the Stone's strong historical association with Scone has prompted modern claims that 'Stone of Scone' is its 'correct' name, although it is over 700 years since the Stone was there. But, despite its antiquity, 'Stone of Scone' was revived as a name only in the mid-nineteenth century. Nevertheless, this was the Stone's preferred name in Scotland throughout much of the twentieth century, emphasising the Stone's significance to the Scots. Until the Stone's return to Scotland in 1996, 'Stone of Scone' was, to some Scots, a defiant reminder of the injustice (real or perceived) of the Stone's continued absence from both its historic location of Scone and Scotland. But 'Stone of Scone' also has extensive academic and official approval and was used in the royal warrant authorising the Stone's restoration.

In England, the Stone was widely known as Jacob's Stone or Pillow from the late-sixteenth century. This reflects the myth, first recorded by Rishanger, that Jacob used this stone as a pillow when he dreamt of angels ascending to heaven. But some writers were sceptical. William Camden's *Reges, Reginae, Nobiles* (1600) referred to 'the Stone of Jacob (*Saxo Iacobi*), as they call it', while in 1719 John Toland noted that the Stone 'tis now by the vulgar call'd JACOB-STONE, as if this had been JACOB'S pillow at Bethel'. But the name's popular appeal, and the myth that inspired it, ensured its survival into the 1950s.

Throughout the twentieth century, the Stone was widely known, particularly in England, as the 'Coronation Stone', from the central role it has played in the coronations of firstly English, and subsequently British, monarchs. 'Coronation Stone' carries very different ideological associations from the 'Stone of Scone', stressing the Stone's seemingly

1 *The 'Sacred Scone of Scotland'.* As illustrated by John Reynolds in W.C. Sellar and R.J. Yeatman's *1066 and All That: a Memorable History of England* (1930)

permanent presence in Westminster Abbey, the setting of those royal rituals, and its physical dislocation from Scone and the Scots. 'Coronation Stone', therefore, was less popular in Scotland, where its use was restricted largely to formal or official use; although William Skene's 1869 study was titled *The Coronation Stone*, the name appears in the text only twice.

Attempts to reconcile the Stone's varied historical associations have resulted in several unconvincing hybrid names, including the 'Coronation Stone of Scotland', 'Scottish Coronation Stone' and 'Coronation Stone of Destiny'. And, in a comic departure from tradition, the Stone is memorably referred to as the 'Sacred Scone of Scotland' in W.C. Sellar and R.J. Yeatman's *1066 and All That* (1930) (**1**).

THE PROPHECY

Some of the Stone's most popular names have been derived from the prophecy associated with it. Although the Stone is now most widely known as the 'Stone of Destiny', this is an obscure and yet relatively recent name, in use only since the mid-nineteenth century. Inspired by mythology, this name reflects the extent to which these sources have dominated the Stone's popular perception. The origin of the name requires explanation.

Although the Stone of Destiny is a modern name, its origins lie in a medieval prophecy that is central to the Stone's mythology from the earliest recorded appearance of the tradition. *Liber Extravagans* attributes the prophecy to Milo, mythical king of the Scots in Spain. Giving the Stone to Simon Brecc, his favoured son, on Simon's departure for Ireland:

> Milo prophesied to his son, who, on being strengthened
> when he received this Stone, began to rejoice,
> that his descendants would reign wherever he placed it.

A version of this prophecy was known in England around the same time. *La Piere d'Escoce* relates how Moses prophesied to the Scots, before they left Egypt with the Stone, that 'Whoever will possess this stone / Shall be the conqueror of a very far-off land'. This, and Rishanger's version of the Stone's mythical origins, expresses the prophecy's political significance from a specifically English perspective. The prophecy did not retain the same meaning throughout the Middle Ages, but was either modified to suit specific political circumstances, or perceived differently according to its context.

That the prophecy was invested with political significance is apparent from the occasions on which it was recited. When the Scots demanded the Stone's return in 1324, they claimed that 'Moses had prophesied that whoever bore that stone with him should bring broad lands under the yoke of his lordship', according to the *Life of Edward II*. Referring to the coronation of David II in 1331, the *Chronicles of Melsa* state that the Stone was brought to Scotland because 'Moses ... prophesied [that] a prince who would acquire many islands would sit upon that throne'. But, seeking to exonerate Edward I from any blame for seizing a symbol that Moses had linked specifically with the fortunes of the Scots, the chronicler pointedly added: 'But this Prince David himself was not the one of whom the prophecy was made; nor did he deserve to sit upon this stone'.

The origins of the prophecy are obscure, although it is integral to the Stone's mythology. The prophecy appears to originate in early Scottish mythology and perhaps originally referred to the assimilation of the Picts, the indigenous inhabitants of what is now north-eastern Scotland, by the Scots from the mid-ninth century. The tradition of the Scots migrating with the Stone that symbolised their kingship, from Ireland to Argyll and then to Scone, may have been one strategy the Scots deployed in an attempt to legitimise the extension of their power over the Picts.

Alternatively, the prophecy may have been inspired by the Stone's seizure in 1296. While Edward's possession of the Stone symbolised English overlordship of Scotland, the Scots may have responded with their own counter-propaganda, prophesing that Scottish kings would rule wherever the Stone was kept, including England. Indeed, the prophecy may have been invested with political significance in more than one historical context; the Stone's removal from Scone may have given an already ancient prophecy a new lease of life. Regardless of its origins, the prophecy clearly carried a potent political message.

The prophecy's most detailed version is in John of Fordun's *Chronicle of the Scottish People*. Although compiled in the 1370s, Fordun's account of the Scots' mythical origins was based on sources which were already in existence by 1301. Fordun relates how Simon Brec raised the Stone from the sea off the Irish coast:

> So he accepted this stone as a precious gift bestowed on him by the gods and as a sure omen that he would be king. And, beside himself with excessive joy, he gave solemn thanks to his gods with such great fervour, as if they had handed both the kingdom and the crown over to him unconditionally. He also recited

there a prophecy about it from his gods ... that in future, in whatsoever kingdom or lordship they found the stone after it had been forcibly removed from them through the power of their enemies, the prophets bade them regard it as certain that they and their descendants would reign thereafter in that same place.

Underlining the prophecy's political nature, the reference to the Stone's removal by force was presumably prompted by the actions of Edward I, giving the prophecy added relevance in a new historical context.

Fordun then summarised the prophecy in an unattributed leonine couplet:

this has been expressed in prophetic verse as follows:
If destiny deceives not, the Scots will reign 'tis said
In that same place where the stone has been laid.
(*Ni fallat fatum, Scoti quocumque locatum*
Invenient lapidem, regnare tenentur ibidem.)

And this, according to the claims of popular opinion up to the present day, is shown to have been true on many occasions in the early wanderings of the Scots. For they themselves regained by force this stone that had been seized by their enemies, both Spanish chieftains and the native Irish, together with their territories as in the prophecy given above.

Fordun's versions of the prophecy had an enduring influence on the Stone's mythology and symbolism. Both the prophecy and couplet were incorporated in successive Scottish chronicles, although their forms vary widely as a result of poetic licence.

Andrew of Wyntoun's *Orygynale Cronykil*, composed between 1408 and 1424 (probably 1420–24), contains the earliest extant translation of the prophetic couplet into Scots. This refers to the Stone's 'werdis' (weird), its fate or destiny:

Now I wil the worde rahers	*Now will I the word rehearse*
As I fynde of that stane in wersse:	*As I find of that Stone in verse:*
'Bot gif that werdis failzeande be,	*'But if that destiny false be,*
Qwhar euir that stane ze segit se,	*Wherever that Stone sitting you see,*
Thar sal the Scottis be regnande,	*There shall the Scots be regnant*
And lordis hail our all that lande'.	*And lords whole over all that land'.*

The prophecy's political significance is evident in Blind Harry's (*fl.* 1470–92) metrical life of Sir William Wallace:

Quhar that stayne is Scottis suld mastir be.	*Where this stone is Scots shall masters be.*
God ches the tyme Margretis ayr till see!	*God choose the time Margaret's heir to see!*

St Margaret, queen of Malcolm III (1057–93), was the ancestress of both the Scottish and English royal lines, through her sons and daughters respectively. Harry overtly expresses the Stone's symbolic and nationalistic significance. By taking the Stone on which the Scottish kings were inaugurated, Edward had unwittingly initiated a chain of predestined events. This had already led to the descendants of Scottish kings holding the English crown and would, on the prophecy's fulfilment, deliver the English crown to Scottish kings.

Quoting Fordun's prophetic couplet, Hector Boece's *Scotorum Historiae* (1527) claimed that 'after long ages (as the thing itself indicates) this inscription was carved upon the Stone'. The translation of Boece's *History* into Scots resulted in the wider dissemination of the Stone's mythology and prophecy. The prose translation by John Bellenden, *Croniklis of the Scots* (1531), related how Gathelus, king of the Scots in Spain:

> sittand in his chiar of merbill, within his ciete of Brigance, governit his pepill, in justice. This chiar of merbill had sic weird, that it made every land, quhair it wes found, native to Scottis; as thir versis schawis:
> 'The Scottis sall bruke that realme as native ground,
> Gif weirdes faill nocht, quhair evir this chiar is found'.
> Throw quhilkis happnit, that the said chiar of merbill wes eftir brocht out of Spayne in Ireland; and out of Ireland in thay partis of Albion, quhilk wer callit eftir Scotland. In this chiar all kingis of Scotland war ay crownit.
> (*sitting in his chair of marble within his city of Brigance, governed his people in justice. This chair of marble had such a prophecy, that it made every land where it was found, native to the Scots, as this verse shows:*
> '*The Scots shall hold that realm as native ground,*
> *If fates fail not, wherever this chair is found*'.
> *Through which happened, that the said chair of marble was later brought out of Spain into Ireland; and out of Ireland into those parts of Albion, which were later called Scotland. In this chair all kings of Scotland were always crowned*)

The verse translation, William Stewart's *Buik of the Croniclis of Scotland* (*c*.1535), describes the greeting Fergus, the mythical first king of the Scots of Scotland, received on arriving in Scotland with the Stone:

> Than lord and lord, and bald barroun and knycht,
> And all the laif with ane loud voce on hicht,
> 'Fergus', tha said, 'and his successioun,
> In heretage sall euer bruke this croun'.
> Syne war all suorne to keip that leill and trew;
> For moir effect, in greit lettres of grew,
> Grauit this thing intill ane mekill stane,
> Weill gilt with gold as it suld neuir be gane.
> (*Then lord and lord, and bold baron and knight,*
> *And all the rest with one loud voice on high,*
> '*Fergus*', *they said*, '*and his succession,*
> *In heritage shall ever hold this crown*'.
> *Then all were sworn to keep that loyal and true;*
> *For more effect, in great letters of Greek,*

Engraved this thing onto a large stone,
Well gilded with gold as it should never be gone.)

Raphael Holinshed's *Chronicles of England, Scotland and Ireland* (1577) introduced medieval Scottish traditions to an English audience for the first time, stimulating interest in the Stone and its prophecy. Philemon Holland's translation of William Camden's *Britannia* (1610) gave the earliest English rendition of the prophecy:

Except old fawes be vaine,
And wits of wisards blind:
The Scots in place must raigne:
Where they this stone shall finde.

But perhaps the best known translation of Fordun's prophetic couplet is by Sir Walter Scott, in his *History of Scotland* (1830):

Unless the fates are faithless found,
And prophets' voice be vain,
Where'er this monument is found
The Scottish race shall reign.

Regardless of its origins and precise translation, the prophecy has long been intimately associated with the Stone.

THE STONE OF DESTINY

The Stone of Destiny, as the Stone is now most popularly known, owes its name to the prophecy or destiny associated with it. But although the prophecy was in existence at the start of the fourteenth century, the name did not appear until the late-sixteenth. Its development may be traced from Boece's *History*. Employing 'fatal' in its now archaic sense of 'fateful' or 'destiny', Boece referred to the 'fatal stone in the form of a throne' (*lapis cathedrae instar fatalis*), which Bellenden's translation rendered as 'fatale chiar'. Drawing on Bellenden's account, Holinshed's *Chronicles* referred to the prophecy as a 'destiny': 'This stone ... having such a fatal destinie, as the Scottes say, following it, that wheresoever it should be founde, there shoulde the Scottish men raigne and have the supreme governance'.

The Stone was soon referred to by the 'destiny' associated with it. It is the 'Chyre of Destinie' in J. Dalrymple's *Historie of Scotland* (1596), translated from Jhone Leslie's *De Origine, Moribus et Rebus Gestis Scotorum* (1578), which explains that 'in this chyre, quhilke our cuntrey people called of Destenie, all our Scottis kings ... used to be crouned'. A marginal note added that 'The marmor [marble] chyre is the Scottis chyre of destinie or gude luck'. The 'Chair of Destiny' is synonymous with the 'Stone of Destiny'; in accordance with mythological convention, the *Historie of Scotland* describes a 'marmore stane in [the] forme of a chyre'.

'Chair of Destiny' did not catch on as a name and the Stone continued to be known in Scotland as the 'fatal stone' and 'fatal chair'. Although sometimes descriptive, they were also proper names: the 'Fatal Stone' and 'Fatal Chair'. These names were used widely until c.1870, after which they declined, although W. Douglas Simpson was still using them as late as 1958.

There was also some scepticism about the validity of 'Fatal Stone' as a name; Toland refers to 'the FATAL STONE so call'd'. Attesting confusion, many commentators referred to the Stone by more than one name. For example, reporting Queen Victoria's coronation in 1837, the *Sun* referred to the Stone 'commonly called Jacob's, or the fatal Marble'. Some nineteenth-century names, such as *Saxum fatale*, are deliberate archaisms, while the 'famous stone' recalls medieval references. Increased interest in the Stone during the late eighteenth and nineteenth centuries occurred before a widely accepted name for it had emerged, when there was still a tendency to refer to the Stone descriptively. It was often described then as the 'palladium' of the Scots; the Stone was believed to have protective qualities, safeguarding the destiny of the Scottish people.

As 'Fatal Stone' became increasingly archaic and obscure, related but more readily understandable names, including 'fated stone', 'fateful stone' and 'Stone of Fate', appeared from the 1830s. These names conveyed more overtly the perceived significance of 'the stone on which the fate of Scotland might be said to hang', as Joseph Hunter explained in 1856. From there, it was only a small step to 'Stone of Destiny'.

But the emergence of 'Stone of Destiny' as a name was influenced by a confusion with another stone. Medieval chronicles relating how the Stone was kept at Tara in Ireland before being brought to Scotland led to its identification with the *Lia Fáil* (Irish, 'Stone of Destiny') at Tara, Co. Meath. According to early Irish mythology, the *Lia Fáil* screamed when the rightful king of Tara stood on it and is traditionally, but questionably, identified with a stone that still stands at Tara (**colour plate 1**). This confusion resulted in the Scottish Stone also being referred to as the *Lia Fáil*, as it still is occasionally, and, more rarely, as the 'Stone of Destiny', as in Dr Ferdinando Warner's *The History of Ireland* (1763). Although the Stone of Destiny and *Lia Fáil* are separate stones, their confusion was influential in the mid-nineteenth century adoption of the name 'Stone of Destiny' for the Stone then in Westminster Abbey.

Although not used continuously, two of the Stone's commonest names are of considerable antiquity. The earliest reference to the Stone of Scone is in 1327. And although 'Stone of Destiny', the name now most widely associated with the Stone, has been in general use only since the mid-nineteenth century, 'Chair of Destiny' dates from 1596. The origins of this name are much older, lying in the prophecy that has been associated with the Stone since at least 1296–1306. 'Stone of Destiny' is now so well established and widely accepted as a name that to abandon it would not only be pointless and confusing, but would also deny the significance of the prophecy which has been intimately associated with the Stone throughout its recorded history.

2

MYTHICAL ORIGINS

Respecting the real history of this talisman, it is now in vain to inquire.
John MacCulloch, *A Description of the Western Isles of Scotland* (1819)

The origins of the Stone of Destiny are shrouded in myth. The best known form of this myth was summarised by Thomas Pennant, the antiquarian, naturalist and traveller, writing of his Scottish tour in 1772:

> In the church of this abbey [Scone] was preserved the famous chair, whose bottom was the fatal stone, the palladium of the Scottish monarchy; the stone, which had first served Jacob for his pillow, was afterwards transported into Spain, where it was used as a seat of justice by Gethalus, contemporary with Moses. It afterwards found its way to Dunstaff[n]age in Argyleshire, continued there as the coronation chair till the reign of Kenneth II [Cináed mac Alpín], who to secure his empire removed it to Scone. Here it remained, and in it every Scottish monarch was inaugurated till the year 1296, when Edward I, to the mortification of North-Britain, translated it to Westminster Abbey; and with it, according to ancient prophecy, the empire of Scotland.

This brief account encompasses the myth's essential elements: the Stone's origins, travels and significance, and the prophecy associated with it. Whether it is believed or not, this myth remains essentially unchanged to this day and is repeated in countless popular histories.

William Skene, Historiographer Royal for Scotland and pioneering historian of Celtic Scotland, made the first attempt to distinguish between the Stone's mythology and history. In 1869, Skene bemoaned that:

> the legend of the Stone of Destiny ... has taken such hold of the Scottish mind, that it is less easily dislodged from its place in the received history of the country; and there it still stands, in all its naked improbability, a solitary waif from the sea of myth and fable, with which modern criticism has hardly ventured to meddle, and which modern scepticism has not cared to question.

Little has changed since then. The myths surrounding the Stone are powerful and enduring, ingrained upon Scottish consciousness and famous around the world.

The Stone's mythical origins are more complex than Pennant indicated. Many versions of the myth exist and Pennant's account combines elements from these into a composite 'super myth'. In the absence of a documented early history for the Stone, mythology has filled the void. The frequent confusion of myth and history has profoundly influenced the popular perception of the Stone's origins, obscuring the myths' historical significance and the medieval perceptions they reflect. Mythology is central to understanding the Stone. This chapter examines the Stone's mythical origins, tracing the evolution of the myth through a wide range of medieval sources before looking at the origins and function of the myths themselves. The chapter concludes by looking at the Stone's modern mythology.

THE EVOLUTION OF THE MYTH

The Stone of Destiny features in an extensive body of medieval mythology concerning the origins of the Scots. Although none of these myths survive in texts that pre-date the Stone's removal from Scone in 1296, Dr Dauvit Broun has shown that the Scottish origin myths in some fourteenth- and fifteenth-century chronicles are closely based on versions belonging to 1292–1306. This attests the existence of a developed body of mythology concerning the Stone at the time it was removed from Scone. And, indicating that these myths may be considerably earlier, they are ultimately derived from a common source, an origin myth with an appended king list.

The earliest surviving mythological reference to the Stone is in Baldred Bisset's *Processus* (1301):

> The daughter of Pharaoh, king of Egypt, landed in Ireland with an armed force and a very large fleet of ships. Then, after taking on board some Irishmen, she sailed to Scotland, carrying with her the royal seat ... She conquered and overthrew the Picts, and took over that kingdom. And from this Scota the Scots and Scotland take their name; hence the verse: 'The whole of Scotland is named after the woman Scota'.

Bisset's account of Scottish origins is a model of conciseness. Other versions are more detailed, but their narratives are fragmented, with missing and/or duplicated episodes. This attests their piecemeal construction from earlier sources and the existence of several textual versions of the myth at the start of the fourteenth century.

Scalacronica ('Ladder Chronicle') was compiled by Sir Thomas Grey of Heton from sources he had access to while imprisoned by the Scots in Edinburgh Castle in 1355–63. But the passage concerning the Stone quotes from a text which can be dated to 1292–1304:

> In which Isle [Ireland] afterwards arrived Symond Bret, the youngest son of the king of Spain, who brought with him a stone, on which the kings of Spain were accustomed to be crowned, which his father gave him as a token that he was made king of it, as the one whom he loved most of his children. This Symond became king of the country of Ireland ... who placed the foresaid stone in the most sovereign beautiful place of the country, called to this day the Royal Place.

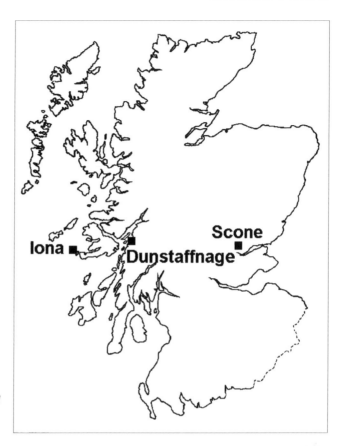

2 *Scotland, showing places associated with the mythical travels of the Stone of Destiny.* Nick Aitchison

The abridged nature of this account is apparent from its claim that the Stone was then moved directly from Ireland to Scone: 'Fergus brought out of Ireland the royal stone ... and placed it where is now the Abbey of Scone'.

Liber Extravagans includes the details, omitted by *Scalacronica*, of the Stone's transfer from Ireland to Scotland; 'a bold warrior called Fergus brought the Stone to Argyll':

> He was the first to rule the Scots, because he brought the Stone.
> The Scots decreed to set up this Stone as the throne of kings,
> but only of their own kings, not alien kings.
> As Scone bears witness, that Stone was until then placed there.

This may reflect the tradition that the kingdom of the Scots – in the form of the kingdom of Dál Riata, traditionally founded by Irish migrants in the fifth century – originated in Argyll (**2**). Reflecting alternative accounts of the Stone's origins, *Liber Extravagans* also refers to the Stone as the Pharaoh's Stone (*'lapidem Pharaonis'*) and the 'anchor of life' (*anchora vite*).

John of Fordun, probably a chantry priest in Aberdeen Cathedral, compiled his

Chronicle of the Scottish People (*Chronica Gentis Scotorum*) sometime between 1371 and 1377. Fordun collected source material 'in the meadow of Britain and among the oracles of Ireland, through cities and towns, through universities and colleges, through churches and monasteries, talking with historians and visiting chronographers', according to the 'Book of Cupar Angus' version of Bower's *Scotichronicon*. Fordun encountered problems in constructing a continuous historical narrative from diverse and sometimes contradictory sources, usually cited only as 'a chronicle' or 'another chronicle'. Fordun's practice of lifting passages directly from these sources is responsible for the disjointed nature of his *Chronicle*. But Fordun was a diligent researcher and his *Chronicle* preserves accounts of the Stone's origins that were in existence by 1301 and have not survived elsewhere.

Fordun's *Chronicle* contains two contradictory versions of the myth. Presumably unable to decide between them, Fordun included both:

> ... there was a king of the Scots in Spain called Milo, who had several sons. Although he was not the oldest, nor the heir, yet he loved one of them, whose name was Simon Brecc, more than all the others. So his father sent him to Ireland with an army, and presented him with a marble throne of very ancient workmanship, carved by a careful craftsman, on which the kings of the Scottish people in Spain used to sit. So it was kept carefully in its own particular place, to be, as it were, an anchor. Now this Simon Brecc set out for the aforesaid island accompanied by a great crowd of people and, after subduing it under his rule, he reigned there for many years. He placed the aforesaid stone, that is, the throne, in a place in his kingdom of some height which was called Tara. For the future, this was to be his royal seat and the chief place in his kingdom, and there the kings descended from his line used to have their seat throughout many ages, adorned with the insignia of royalty.
>
> One story is that Gaythelos took this seat with him from Egypt to Spain together with the other regalia; but others say that Simon Brecc let down anchors from his ship and secured them in the sea near the Irish coast. When he was forced by adverse winds to pull them up again from the stormy waves, he only just managed to do so with the utmost possible effort, and along with the anchors he raised from the depths of the sea and pulled into the ship a block of marble cut in the shape of a throne.

Tara, Co Meath, is *Scalacronica*'s 'Royal Place'. Tara has strong royal associations, mythical and historical, as the seat and/or assembly place of the kingship of Tara and the high-kingship of Ireland (3). The Stone's mythological association with Tara reflects this. If the Stone was kept in Ireland, Scottish chroniclers probably reasoned, Tara was the obvious location. But the Stone may also have been linked with Tara to enhance its royal associations and symbolic significance and, by association, the status of the Scottish kingship. This suggests the origin of this tradition before the Stone was seized in 1296.

In contrast to its arrival in Ireland, Fordun's description of how the Stone reached Scotland is uncharacteristically terse:

3 *Tara, Co. Meath, from the air. These earthworks lie at the centre of an extensive prehistoric ritual complex and early medieval royal centre. According to mythology, the Stone of Destiny was kept here before being taken to Scotland. The stone pillar commonly known as the* Lia Fáil *formerly stood on the Mound of the Hostages, a Neolithic passage tomb (centre), but is now on the mound towards the left.* Copyright: Cambridge University Committee for Aerial Photography

there came from Ireland a certain king called Fergus son of Feradach, who later brought to Scotland the royal throne carved out of marble, on which the Scots crowned their first king in Scotland.

Fordun's account is also incomplete; he does not reveal where Fergus, 'first king of Scots in the island', kept the Stone in Scotland or explain how it reached Scone. Some manuscripts attribute this passage to the *History of the Blessed Congall* (*Historia Beati Congalli*). Congall may be St Comgall, who founded the monastery of Bangor, Co Down, in the sixth century. But, emphasising Fordun's importance for preserving texts which have since been lost, this passage does not appear in the surviving *Life of Comgall* or any other source.

Andrew of Wyntoun was Prior of St Serf's, an island monastic community in Loch Leven, Kinross-shire. Wyntoun's *Orygynale Cronykil*, composed in metrical verse sometime between 1408 and 1424, derived its account of the Stone from the same common source as *Scalacronica* and Fordun's *Chronicle*. Wyntoun relates how a king of Spain sent his son, Symon Brek, to Ireland:

A gret stane the kynge than hade,	*A great stone the king then had,*
That for this kyngis set was made,	*That for this king's seat was made,*
And haldyn was a gret iowalle	*And was holding a great jewel*

Withe in the kynrik of Spanzhe hail.	*Within the kingdom of Spain whole.*
This kynge bad this Symon ta	*This king bade this Symon to*
That stane and in til Irland ga,	*That stone and into Ireland go,*
And wyn that lande and occupy,	*And win that land and occupy,*
And halde that stane perpetually,	*And hold that stone perpetually,*
And mak it his seigis thar,	*And make it his throne there,*
As thai of Spanzhe did of it aire.	*As they of Spain did before.*
This Symon did than as the kynge	*This Symon then did as the king*
Fully gaf hym in biddynge,	*Fully gave him in bidding,*
And wan Irlande and chesit his plasse	*And won Ireland and chose his place*
Qwhar honest and mast likly was,	*Where honest and most likely was,*
Thar he made a gret cite,	*There he made a great city,*
And in it syne that stane gert he	*And in it then that stone took he*
Be haldyn and set for iowalle	*Beholden and set for a jewel*
And chartyr of that kynrik haile.	*And charter of that kingdom whole.*
Fergus Erchson fra hym syne	*Fergus, Erc's son, from him then*
Down descendande ewyn be lyne	*Was descended line by line*
In to the fyfe and fifty gre,	*Over generations five and fifty,*
As ewyn reknande men may se,	*As even-reckoning men may see,*
Broucht this stane within Scotlande,	*Brought this stone into Scotland,*
First quhen he come and wan that lande	*First when he came and won that land;*
And set it first in Icolmkyll,	*And set it on Iona first,*
And Scone thar eftyr it was broucht til.	*And later it to Scone was brought.*

That the Stone was kept on Iona (Gaelic, *Í Colm Cille*) when it was first brought to Scotland is not recorded elsewhere. But Iona must have been an obvious contender and its appearance in the myth has a geographical and historical inevitability. A small island off the west coast of Scotland, Iona was where St Columba founded a monastery in 563 (**4**) and played a prominent role in the subsequent conversion to Christianity of northern Scotland. Iona also had strong royal connections: early Scottish kings were buried there. However, despite a popular nineteenth-century tradition that the Stone was 'St Columba's Pillow', there is no evidence that it was ever on Iona.

La Piere d'Escoce, composed shortly after Edward I's death in 1307, is the earliest reference to the Stone in an English source:

What the Stone of Scotland is, I tell you for truth,
 On which the Kings of Scotland were placed in their seat.
 John Balliol was the last, according to what is told,
 Who received his dignity on this stone.

Now Edward, King of England, has conquered it,
 By the grace of Jesus Christ and by hard warfare.
 He offers it to Saint Edward like a king of great importance.
 Now he has passed by death, that no one can avoid.

4 *Iona Abbey from the air. The site of the sixth-century foundation of St Columba, where the Stone of Destiny is reputed to have been kept when first brought to Scotland. The restored thirteenth-century abbey sits within an area enclosed by the sweeping arc of the early medieval monastic earthworks (foreground).* Copyright: Royal Commission on the Ancient and Historical Monuments of Scotland

In Egypt, Moses preached to the people,
Scota, Pharaoh's daughter, listened well,
For he said in the spirit, 'Whoso will possess this stone,
Shall be the conqueror of a very far-off land'.

Gaidelon and Scota brought this stone,
When they passed from the land of Egypt to Scotland,
Not far from Scone, when they arrived.
They named the land Scotland from Scota's name.

After Scota's death her husband took no other wife,
But made his dwelling in the land of Galloway.
From his own name he gave Galloway its name.
Thus it appears that Scotland and Galloway are derived from their names.

Now has Edward passed from this life,
The conqueror of lands and flower of chivalry.
Let us pray almighty God, who sways the whole world,
That God may have mercy on his soul, God the son of Mary.

La Piere d'Escoce is based on a Scottish account of the Stone's mythical origins but omits the Stone's travels. Instead, the Stone was brought directly from Egypt to an unidentified place near Scone, without any reference to Spain, Ireland or Argyll. This reflects the composer's freedom from the conventions surrounding Scottish versions of the myth. Indeed, the irrelevant detail about Gaidelon not remarrying reveals that *La Piere d'Escoce* was unevenly abridged from a longer account. *La Piere d'Escoce* mistakenly derives Galloway from Gaidelon's name.

The *Life of Edward II* contains a brief account of the Stone's mythical origins which is ultimately derived from Scottish sources: 'Scota, daughter of Pharaoh, brought this stone with her from the borders of Egypt when she landed in Scotland and subdued the land .... Whence from Scota the land is called Scotland'. But another English source, William of Rishanger's *Chronica et Annales* (*c.*1327), departs radically from Scottish myths. Attributing a Biblical origin to the 'regal stone', Rishanger claimed this was Jacob's Pillow. Without any reference to Scotland or the Scots, it is most unlikely that Rishanger, a monk of St Albans, heard this from a Scottish source.

Blind Harry's *The Wallace* referred to the Stone seized by Edward I in 1296 as:

that sammyne stane	*that same stone,*
At Gadalos send with his sone fra Spane, Spaine	*That Gadalos sent with his son from Spain*
Quhen Iber Scot fyrst in-till Irland come.	*When Iber Scot first into Ireland came.*
At Canmor syne king Fergus has it nome,	*From Tara then King Fergus has it taken,*
Brocht it till Scwne and stapill maid it, thar there,	*Brought it to Scone, and stable made it*
Quhar kingis was cround viii hundyr hundred	*Where kings were crowned for eight*
yer and mar	*years and more,*
Before the tyme at king Eduuard it fand.	*Before the time that King Edward found it.*

Harry's claim that kings were crowned on the Stone at Scone for over 800 years before its removal would mean, if correct, that the Stone had been at Scone since before 500.

The myth was embellished by Hector Boece (1465–1536), regent master in arts and later principal of King's College, Aberdeen's new university, in his *Scotorum Historiae* (1527). Boece's lengthy account may be summarised as follows:

Gathelus, an Athenian or Argive, travelled from Greece to Egypt, where he married Scota, daughter of Pharaoh. At the Exodus, Gathelus fled with Scota to Iberia, where he founded a kingdom at Brigantium, now Santiago de Compostela. There, Gathelus reigned in the marble chair, or fatal stone like a chair: wherever it was found would be the kingdom of the Scots. Simon Breck, a descendant of Gathelus, then took the chair from Spain to Ireland, and was crowned king of Ireland in it.

Fergus son of Ferchard, the first king of the Scots in Scotland, moved the chair from Ireland to Argyll, and was crowned in it. In Argyll, he founded the town of *Beregonium*, and placed the Stone in it. Forty Scottish kings were descended from

Fergus. The twelfth king, Evenus, founded the town of *Evonium*, near *Beregonium*. The Stone was moved to *Evonium*, where the rest of the forty kings were crowned, reigned, and were buried.

The Scots were expelled to Ireland during the reign of the last of those forty kings, but returned to Scotland under Fergus mac Erc, who was crowned in the marble chair. Fergus founded a church on Iona, and this became the burial place of the Scottish kings.

Kenneth mac Alpín, the descendant of these kings, conquered the Picts, and moved the Stone from Argyll to Scone, because this was where he won his main victory over the Picts.

The Stone's travels to and fro across the North Channel enable conflicting traditions about the first king of the Scots in Scotland to be reconciled. *Beregonium* and *Evonium* are both mythical places and first appear in Boece's *History*. *Evonium* allegedly owed its name to the town's founder, Evenus or Ewen, (mythical) twelfth king of the Scots, but the burial there of the first forty (mythical) Scottish kings indicates that it was modelled on Iona. *Beregonium* was spuriously derived from *Rerigonium*, in the Rhinns of Galloway, recorded by Ptolemy in the second century.

Boece added a new element to the myth, that Kenneth moved the Stone from Argyll to Scone. After periods of strife between the Scots and Picts, and the intermarriage of their royal dynasties, Kenneth occupied the Pictish kingship, an event traditionally dated to 843. A process of assimilation culminated around 900 in the forging of a new political and territorial unit and identity, comprising eastern Scotland between the rivers Forth and Spey. This was known in Gaelic as *Alba* and, later, in Latin as *Scotia*, the embryonic kingdom of the Scots. The eclipse of Pictish power explained how the Stone got from Argyll to Scone; the Scottish powerbase shifted eastwards to occupy the Pictish political heartland of southern Perthshire, including the royal centre of Scone. Interweaving myth and history, Boece linked the conclusion of the Stone's travels with the founding of the Scottish kingdom.

Boece's colourful narrative and lively literary style ensured that his *History* had an enduring influence on the Scots' perception of their past. This was assisted by its translation into Scots, in both prose and verse, commissioned by James V. John Bellenden's *Croniklis of Scotland* and William Stewart's *Buik of the Croniclis of Scotland* were completed between 1531 and 1535. Both contain some material that is not in Boece or in each other.

Bellenden's and Stewart's translations form the basis of popular traditions concerning the Stone that survives to this day. Notably, Bellenden substituted Dunstaffnage at the mouth of Loch Etive, Argyll, for *Evonium*. Built in the mid-thirteenth century by the MacDougall Lords of Lorne, Dunstaffnage was one of the most impressive castles in western Scotland (**5**) and an obvious candidate for *Evonium*. Boece's Evenus may be based on Ewen, who possibly built the castle and probably died in 1275. The earlier history of Dunstaffnage is obscure, but there is no evidence that it was ever a royal centre. Nevertheless, Dunstaffnage entered popular tradition as the ancient Scottish capital, where the Stone was first kept in Scotland. Dunstaffnage still features prominently in the Stone's mythology.

5 *Dunstaffnage Castle, Lorne, Argyll. Although the present castle dates from the thirteenth to sixteenth centuries, medieval chroniclers claimed that this was where the Scots kept the Stone of Destiny when they first arrived in Scotland.* Copyright: Royal Commission on the Ancient and Historical Monuments of Scotland

At the end of a long sequence of medieval traditions, Boece, Bellenden and Stewart were responsible for the culmination of the Stone's mythology, its wide dissemination and lasting popularity. This appeal is due partly to the rich descriptions of characters and events and their association with known locations. Boece and his translators introduced important new elements to the myth, features which remain central to popular traditions concerning the Stone. But medieval accounts of the Stone are mythological in nature; they do not concern 'real' historical events and no reliability can be attached to their contents.

THE ORIGINS OF THE MYTH

The myth of the Stone of Destiny belongs to the origin myth of the Scots themselves: it describes where the Scots and their Stone came from and how they reached Scotland (**colour plate 2**). It also explains how Scotland and the Scots received their names from the eponymous Scota, while the Gaels, the Gaelic-speaking inhabitants of Scotland, derived their name from Scota's husband, Gaythelos (Gaelic, Gaedhil Glas). The Stone's mythical travels from Ireland to Argyll, and from there to Scone, also mirror the traditions of the Scots' migration from north-eastern Ireland to found the kingdom of Dál Riata during the fifth century, and the Scottish takeover of the Picts in the mid-ninth century.

The most detailed versions of the Scottish origin myth are in the chronicles of Fordun and Boece. Fordun's lengthy and disconnected narrative was derived haphazardly from various unattributed sources and a *Life of St Brendan* but may be reconstructed in summary form:

> In the time of Moses, Gaythelos, son of a Greek king, Neolus, was expelled and travelled to Egypt, where he married Scota, daughter of Pharaoh. After Pharaoh and his army were drowned in the Red Sea, Gaythelos, who had refused to pursue the Jews, was expelled from Egypt, together with his wife and the surviving Greek and Egyptian nobles. Gaythelos, now king of the banished nobles, prepared a fleet to search for new lands 'on the outermost confines of the world'. After travelling in Africa for a considerable time, they crossed to Spain. There they built a town, Brigancia, but the prospect of being defeated by hostile natives led Gaythelos to send a naval expedition to search for unoccupied land. The ships soon reached an island, which they circumnavigated before reporting back to Gaythelos. Gaythelos died shortly after, but first directed his sons to occupy the island. Hyber and Hymec did this, and the island was called Hibernia, after Hyber. Eventually Mycelius became king of the Scots remaining in Spain and sent his sons to take Ireland which, although settled by the Scots in the distant past, was nearly uninhabited. One son, Pertholomus, then occupied Ireland. The third occupation of Ireland was led by Smonbricht, son of the king of the remaining Scots of Spain.

This occupies chapters 8–26 in Book One of Fordun's *Chronicle*. Only then does the Stone appear; its travels, from Spain to Scotland via Ireland, occupy a single chapter, suggesting Fordun's reliance on a separate source for this episode.

Ireland and the Irish feature prominently in the Scottish origin myth. Indeed, Fordun's account reads like an Irish origin myth, with the Scots simply tagged on to the end. It traces the origins of the Irish, describes the discovery, conquest and colonisation of Ireland, and explains how Ireland got its name. Gaythelos is accorded a central role in Ireland's discovery and settlement. Indeed, Gaythelos and Scota are as much eponymous ancestors of the Irish, who were also Gaelic-speaking and were known in Latin as *Scoti* or *Scotti*.

The Irish dimension reveals the cultural and historical contexts of the Scottish origin myth. From its foundation *c*.900, *Alba* shared a common language and culture with Ireland, attested by literary sources, place and personal names, ecclesiastical organisation, saints' cults, sculpture and ornamental metalwork. One of the most impressive expressions of these close cultural links are the round towers of characteristically Irish type at Abernethy (Perthshire) and Brechin (Angus) (**6 and 7**), probably dating from the eleventh century. *Alba* belonged to the wider Gaelic world but formed only a peripheral and relatively recent part of it. The Scots perceived Ireland as their ancestral and cultural homeland and their past as a branch of Irish history.

The Irish identity of the Scots is reflected in their origin myth. The common source from which medieval versions of the myth were ultimately derived predates the emergence of a distinctively Scottish national identity during the War of Independence (1296–1328). But because Fordun's sources date to 1296–1306 and were probably based on even earlier material, the Irish dimension dominates the origin myth, to which the Scottish leg of the odyssey has simply been appended. This distinction disappears in later versions. Bisset's

6 *The round tower of distinctively Irish type at Abernethy, Perthshire. Although the Romanesque belfry windows (one of which is visible near the top of the tower) are of twelfth-century date, the original construction of the tower probably belongs to the eleventh century.* Copyright: Royal Commission on the Ancient and Historical Monuments of Scotland

Processus (1301) attests the refashioning of the myth from a specifically Scottish perspective; Ireland is now relegated to a staging post and source of manpower on the Scots' voyage to Scotland. Now refocused, the myth specifically associated Scota and the *Scoti* with Scotland and the Scots: 'The new name Scotland was given to that part of the island which was thus occupied by the Scots, from that first Scota, the lady of the Scots'. Developing this process, the *Declaration of Arbroath* (1320) omits Ireland from the Scottish origin myth completely.

Origin myths fulfil a deep-seated and universal psychological requirement, explaining a people's place within the world by documenting etymological, genealogical and geographical origins. By tracing the source and route of the Scottish migration, the myth locates the Scots and their land in space. The Scots are also located in time: Fordun dates the kingships of Fergus Mór mac Erc and Kenneth mac Alpín to 1903 and 2349 years after the Scots' exodus from Egypt, which therefore occurred in 1506 BC. Irish and Scottish ecclesiastical scholars strove to fill the void separating their native traditions from Classical and Biblical learning. They did this by synthesising material from their traditions with knowledge derived from the great ecclesiastical scholars Eusebius, Orosius and Isidore of

7 *The round tower at Brechin, Angus. Originally free-standing, the tower is now joined to the thirteenth-century cathedral by a modern aisle. Although the tower is probably eleventh-century in date, the conical roof was probably added in the fourteenth century.* Copyright: Royal Commission on the Ancient and Historical Monuments of Scotland

Seville to form fantastic narratives. This process was underway by the mid-seventh century when Isidore's *Etymologiae* was first studied in Ireland. Isidore's *Etymologiae* concerned the origins of words and names and had a profound influence on Irish literature and thought. It derived the Latin name for Ireland, *Hibernia*, from *Iberia*, leading scholars to conclude that the Irish had come from Spain and to seek their more distant origins. This culminated in the twelfth-century *Book of Invasions of Ireland* (*Lebor Gabála Érenn*), which relates the successive occupations of Ireland by mythological peoples.

The *Book of Invasions* relates the myth of the Irish 'Stone of Destiny', describing how the *Tuatha Dé Danaan* (People of the Goddess Danu/Ana), the fifth mythological people to invade Ireland, brought the *Lia Fáil* to Ireland from the Greek city of Falias, from which the stone supposedly took its name. Indicating the existence of conflicting traditions, the *Book of Invasions* also relates how the Sons of Míl (or Milesians), the sixth and final mythological people to occupy Ireland, brought the *Lia Fáil* from Spain. This confusion is paralleled in Scottish mythology, where the Spanish episode has a different quality and characters from the Stone's earlier travels.

The basic structure and sequence of events in the *Book of Invasions* exhibit similarities to the Scottish origin myth, although there are many differences in their characters and events. But both the Scottish and Irish origin myths may have possessed a common ancestry. Attesting the existence of a version of the myth by the mid-eleventh century, the recension of the *Historia Brittonum* traditionally attributed to 'Nennius' describes how a Scythian noble, husband of Scota, daughter of Pharaoh, was expelled from Egypt after the flight of the Israelites and travelled through Africa and Spain until his descendants reached Dál Riata. Earlier still, Bede's *Historia Ecclesiastica* (731) relates how the Picts sailed from Scythia to Ireland but were not allowed to settle there and so continued to northern Britain. The Scythian connection reveals that the Picts borrowed this myth from the Irish or Scots, who traced the origins of their name, *Scoti*, and therefore their ancestry, to Scythia.

Origin myths comprise a constructed past and can support a particular point of view or advance the interests of a certain group, such as a ruling élite. The Stone's mythology attests its status as a symbol of the Scots' ancient origins and their Irish identity. The Irish connection enables two possible historical contexts for the emergence of a Scottish origin myth, incorporating the Stone, to be identified. The foundation of Dál Riata, traditionally dated to the fifth century, may provide a context for a myth legitimising the newly established kingdom by linking it to its Irish and more distant ancestral homelands. The Picts had certainly appropriated an origin myth of Irish type, possibly from the neighbouring Scots, by 731, while the 'Nennius' recension of the *Historia Brittonum* contains a Dál Riata origin myth.

Alternatively, the myth is associated with the Scottish take-over of Pictland from the mid-ninth century. Drawing on the past, it enhanced the status of the kings of *Alba* by articulating their ancient, auspicious and *Irish* ancestry. This was still evident in 1249, when Alexander III's genealogy was read at his inauguration. Through their origin myth and its associated king list, and by appropriating the Pictish royal centre of Scone, the Scots legitimised their power over the Picts and forged an identity for their newly-founded kingdom of *Alba*. Claiming to have possessed the Stone since time immemorial, and invoking a prophecy that the Scots would reign wherever the Stone was located, the Stone and its mythology were tangible expressions of the new political order, the Scottish domination of the Picts and the creation of *Alba*. Origin myths, Scone and the Stone were central to the ideological strategy employed to legitimise the rule of the early Scottish kings.

MYTHS IN ACTION

Although based on earlier traditions, the earliest surviving versions of the Scottish origin myth belong to a critical point in Scottish history. The death of Alexander III in 1286, followed by that of his only surviving direct heir, his grand-daughter the infant Margaret, Maid of Norway, in 1290, ended the direct line of Scotland's monarchy. Scotland faced a succession crisis that threatened her very existence as an independent kingdom. The interregnum presented Edward I of England with an opportunity. In June 1291, the dozen competitors for the vacant Scottish throne recognised Edward as lord superior of Scotland in return for Edward presiding over the case to determine the rightful succession. The 'Great Cause' was heard at Norham Church, Northumberland, and found in John Balliol's favour in November 1292.

Edward's interference in Scottish affairs and humiliations of Balliol soon precipitated a crisis. A Franco-Scottish alliance (the 'Auld Alliance') was formed in 1295 and the Scots attacked Carlisle Castle unsuccessfully in March 1296. Edward retaliated by taking Berwick-upon-Tweed, massacring its inhabitants, and in April defeated the Scots at Dunbar. Balliol was stripped of his kingship (**colour plate 3**). Edward's subsequent attempt at imposing direct rule over Scotland provoked a popular uprising led by Sir William Wallace and Andrew Moray. Scotland's bitter and protracted War of Independence had begun.

Edward used the past extensively in an attempt to establish a precedent for his claimed overlordship of Scotland. In March and April 1291, chronicles and registers in English monasteries were searched hurriedly, perhaps after royal archives had failed to produce much evidence. In May, Edward presided over a meeting of English magnates and clergy at Norham. This was attended 'by clerks skilled in civil and canon law, and by many monks with their chronicles, in order to reach a conclusion about the overlordship of the realm of Scotland', as Walter of Guisborough recorded. Edward 'summoned monks from some of the churches in England to come with their chronicles'. These chronicles were 'inspected, investigated, and discussed before all the king's council', noted the *Chronicle of Bury St Edmunds*. And, in deciding the Great Cause, 'there were recited articles from chronicles, privileges, and other papal and royal letters, showing that the kings of Scotland had done homage to the kings of England', according to Guisborough.

In June 1299, William Fraser and David Moray, bishops of St Andrews and Moray respectively, used their consecration in Rome to seek Pope Boniface VIII's support for Scottish independence. Boniface's papal bull, *Scimus fili*, challenged Edward to produce evidence of his right of overlordship over Scotland, although it was not received by Edward until August 1300. In November, a search of royal records was ordered and some documents were taken to the parliament at Lincoln in January 1301. This parliament issued letters to English cathedrals and monasteries, again asking them to consult their archives.

Edward's holding response to Boniface in February 1301 was simply to assert that the rights of English kings over Scotland had existed since the time of the Angles and Britons. This was followed by intensive research to prepare a 'historically'-based case. In July, Edward maintained that his argument was based on precedent, the antiquity of England's claimed overlordship of Scotland. This, Edward alleged, originated:

> in the days of Eli and of Samuel the prophet, after the destruction of the city of Troy, a certain valiant and illustrious man of the Trojan race, called Brutus, landed with many noble Trojans upon a certain island called, at that time, Albion. It was then inhabited by giants, and after he had defeated and slain them, by his might and that of his followers, he called it, after his own name, Britain, and his people Britons.

The English claimed descent from Locrine, the eldest son of Brutus and overlord of Brutus' youngest son, Albanact, from whom the Scots were descended. This myth is derived from Geoffrey of Monmouth's *History of the Kings of Britain* (*Historia Regum Britanniae*), which elaborated an episode in the *Historia Brittonum*. English claims were reinforced by a historical account that ended with Balliol's submission to Edward. Although described as an 'appeal to history', there was nothing historical about Edward's claims; instead, the English fabricated a mythological past in an attempt to legitimise and promote contemporary political ambitions.

The Scots were no less inventive in their recourse to a mythological past. Their defence was to document the origins and antiquity of the Scots as an independent nation, combining a counter-attack on English claims with a justification of Scotland's ancient legal right to be free from foreign domination. This they did in a lengthy document, the *Instructiones* (*Instructions*), which formed the basis of Baldred Bisset's *Processus*. Bisset, Professor of Canon Law at Bologna University and a canon of St Andrews Cathedral, was one of three Scots who presented to the Curia, the papal court, the case against Edward's claimed overlordship of Scotland.

Bisset observed that Edward said much but proved little and rebutted the English myths, noting that Edward was of Norman, not ancient British or Trojan, descent. The Scots also rejected their British origins and descent from Brutus and underpinned their claim of independence from English overlordship by invoking their mythical origins as ancient immigrants. Throughout their history the Scots were an independent people and, as they traced their ancestry to Scota, daughter of Pharaoh, 'the Egyptians may claim more right in the kingdom of Scotland than the English'. Moreover, the Scots could document their history as a civilised Christian nation through 36 successive reigns, during which the English were still pagans. Bisset included a Scottish version of the events surrounding Balliol's kingship and concluded with an appeal to universal law, that no kingdom or king should be subject to another. The travels and travails of the Scots, in the face of prolonged hostility from their belligerent and more powerful neighbour, were of Biblical proportions. The Scots cast themselves as God's chosen people and Scotland as their chosen land; God and righteousness were on their side.

The Scots' predicament gave their origin myths renewed relevance. The *Instructiones* explained how 'the ancient Scots travelled from Egypt, and occupied firstly Ireland, then Argyll and, after they had driven the Britons from it, Scotland'. It was to this account that Bisset added a topical reference to the Stone recently taken by Edward. Although this is the earliest surviving incontrovertible reference to the Stone, Bisset is unlikely to have invented the Stone's mythical origins. Few Scottish documentary sources survived the War of Independence or later strife, with the result that any earlier references to the Stone were lost. Moreover, the occurrence by 1292–1306 of an independent account of the myth and the earliest recorded appearance of the prophecy suggests that a version of the myth not only existed but was widely known during the thirteenth century.

But the War of Independence is fundamental to the understanding of the myth's surviving forms. Bisset, prompted by the perilous state of Scottish independence, took an already ancient myth concerning the origins of the Scots and their Stone and adapted it to suit contemporary circumstances. By emphasising the origins and antiquity of the Stone on which Scottish kings were inaugurated, the myth supported the case that Scotland was, and always had been, an independent kingdom. Bisset ingeniously exploited Edward's seizure of the Stone. The Stone symbolised the independence and antiquity of the Scottish kingdom. Its removal by Edward was an explicit recognition of the Stone's symbolic significance to the Scots and, therefore, an implicit acknowledgement of the independence of the Scots and their kingship. Installed in Westminster Abbey, the Stone was incontrovertible material evidence and the principal exhibit in the Scottish case.

During the War of Independence, the prophecy that the Scots would reign wherever the Stone was located assumed a new ideological significance. By removing the Stone to Westminster, Edward was initiating a predestined sequence of events that, according to the prophecy, would eventually lead to the Scots gaining the English crown. The prophecy's propaganda value is obvious: Scottish independence might hang in the balance, but the Scots would emerge victorious in the end. Prophecies featured prominently in medieval thought and it is possible to imagine this one emerging at a time of national crisis. Indeed, it may be compared with similar Scottish prophecies of English defeat circulating *c*.1307.

The case concerning Scottish independence remained unresolved and neither side emerged as victors. Edward died in July 1307, at Burgh-by-Sands on the English side of the Solway Firth, while leading another Scottish campaign. The death of such a formidable opponent, and his succession by the militarily less capable Edward II, encouraged the Scots but even their victory at Bannockburn in 1314 failed to gain English recognition of Scottish independence. Edward still claimed the right of nominating ecclesiastical appointments in Scotland and the Scots' rejection of his nominees led to four Scottish bishops being summoned to appear before Pope John XXII in 1319. In 1320, the Scottish barons sent an *apologia* for the bishops' failure to appear. Better known as the *Declaration of Arbroath*, this includes a synopsis of the Scots' Scythian origins and travels to Scotland, although neither the Stone nor Scota are mentioned. Another version of the Scottish origin myth was used in the Scottish case presented in negotiations held at Bamburgh, Northumberland, in 1321.

The Scots called upon their mythical origins again in the winter of 1324, when peace negotiations at York collapsed after Edward refused to recognise Robert I ('the Bruce') as the independent king of an independent Scotland. The English continued to cite mythology in support of the antiquity and legitimacy of their claimed overlordship of Scotland. In August 1400, Henry IV claimed that the English kings had been lords superior of Scotland since the time of Locrine, son of Brutus. In peace negotiations at Kirk Yetholm, Roxburghshire, in October 1401, the English again recited their myths. But on this occasion the Scots responded not with their own myths, but with 'some very undiplomatic language'. The influence of origin myths in Anglo-Scottish diplomacy was waning, although they remained of interest to medieval chroniclers.

History as we know it today, a rigorous intellectual discipline based on the critical appraisal of source material, did not exist during the Middle Ages. Instead of writing history, chroniclers were engaged in constructing and invoking mythological pasts that supported specific interests. In Scotland, this invariably meant promoting the cause of Scottish independence from English domination. Indeed, the survival of Scottish independence may be attributed to the resistance inspired by a newly-kindled spirit of national identity. In an ethnically and linguistically diverse nation, this identity was created with reference to a mythical past that stressed the origins of the Scots as a free and independent nation.

The past, through the medium of mythology, is malleable and can be adapted to suit specific circumstances. The War of Independence provides the context for the reshaping of politically motivated mythological pasts and the emergence of a distinctively Scottish national identity. For the first time, the origins of the Scots were traced in their own right, instead of simply being treated as an off-shoot of Irish history.

MODERN MYTHS

The mythology surrounding the Stone of Destiny is not confined to the Middle Ages. The appropriation and adaptation of myths ensure their continued relevance, appeal and dissemination. These processes are apparent in modern myths concerning the Stone's origins, functions, historical associations and authenticity. A common characteristic of these is to conflate material from disparate sources – historical and mythological, medieval and modern – to form unique but inevitably unsustainable interpretations.

Modern myths frequently recycle their medieval predecessors by identifying the Stone as Jacob's Pillow or the *Lia Fáil*. Alternatively, they combine previously unassociated elements, linking the Stone with other famous stones and/or early saints to emphasise its great antiquity and sanctity. Pat Gerber claimed that Ireland's famous Blarney Stone is really a fragment of the Stone of Destiny given to Brian Boru, the eleventh-century Irish high-king, as a talisman to assist him in battle. And Marion Campbell's *Argyll: the Enduring Heartland* (1977) stated that:

> Once there was a stone, over which St Patrick prophesied and which later Christian legend made 'Jacob's Pillow'. On it the earliest Christian kings in the British Isles were enthroned, the stone being carried forward as their realm enlarged until it reached Scone ... St Patrick had said ... that wherever it rested the race of Fergus should reign.

These associations are unfounded.

Some modern myths misinterpret medieval sources, projecting the Stone's recorded history back in time. Marion Campbell claimed that the 'Nennius' *Historia Brittonum* describes how Scota, daughter of Pharaoh, brought Jacob's Pillow to Scotland. But although this contains a version of the Scottish origin myth, neither Jacob's Pillow nor the Stone are referred to. According to Jennifer Westwood's *Albion: a Guide to Legendary Britain* (1985), the earliest reference to the Stone is in Robert of Gloucester's (*fl.* 1260–1300) metrical chronicle:

> The Scottes yclupped were
> After a Woman that Scote hyghte, the dawter of Pharaon,
> Yat broghte into Scotlond a whyte marble Ston,

Yat was ordeyned for thure Kyng, whan he coroned wer,
And for a grete Jewyll long hit was yholde ther.

But these lines were only added in the mid-fifteenth century; these allegedly early references to the Stone have no historical basis.

The Stone's appearance in many fictional genres also attests the creation of modern myths. Its earliest portrayal in historical fiction is in Jane Porter's *The Scottish Chiefs: a Romance* (1819). Drawing upon medieval mythology, this described the Stone as 'that holy pillar of Jacob' and 'the sacred gift of Fergus'. One scene describes Wallace's reaction to news that Edward has seized the Stone with the assistance of Scottish collaborators:

Do the traitors think ... that by robbing Scotland of her ... stone, that they really deprive her of her palladium? Fools! Fools! Scotland's history is in the memories of her sons; her palladium is in their hearts; and Edward may one day find that she ... needs not talismans to give her freedom!

In Nigel Tranter's *Kenneth* (1990), Kenneth mac Alpín is firstly crowned and anointed king by the Scots of Dál Riata on the '*Lia Fáil*', the Stone of Destiny, on Iona, where it had been since at least the days of St Columba. After the Scots defeat the Picts in 843, Kenneth transports the Stone across Scotland, from Dunstaffnage to Scone. There, Kenneth is crowned king of *Scotia*, before sitting on the Stone, draped with the Saltire, the Cross of St Andrew. Embellishing Boece's claim that Kenneth transferred it to Scone, Tranter accords the Stone a central and symbolic role at the birth of the Scottish nation.

The publicity surrounding the Stone's removal from Westminster Abbey in 1950–51 and its return to Scotland in 1996 stimulated more fictional appearances by the Stone. The Stone's disputed authenticity is central to Tranter's *The Stone* (1958). T. Houston's romantic thriller, *Wounded Stone* (1998), reflects the Stone's new context. Set in a contemporary revolution, the Stone is hidden in the besieged Edinburgh Castle as a symbol of defiance. Reflecting a long mythical association with the historical Macbeth (1040-57), king of Scots, Robert De Maria's novel, *Stone of Destiny: A Story of Lady Macbeth* (2001), is purportedly based on the life of the historical queen. In contrast, Jim Eldridge's *Captain Hawk and the Stone of Destiny* (1997) introduces the Stone to children's fiction. In this graphical novel, the evil warlord Pinn sends Captain James Hawk and his pessimistic robot Xan-X on a hazardous mission to recover the Stone in only 48 hours. Possession of the Stone gives the power of being able to see into the future, and millions have died trying to obtain it.

The Stone also features in science/fantasy fiction. *The Destiny Stone* (1980) is the third book in Victor Milan and Robert E. Vardeman's 'War of Powers' series. In Patricia Kennealy's *Keltiad* trilogy, set in the year 3512, a spaceship from Earth strays into 'Keltic space'. *Throne of Scone* (1986) takes its title from one of the Treasures of Keltia, an interstellar monarchy whose ancestors left Earth in 453, and is described in *The Copper Crown* (1984) as the great carved stone throne of Aeron Aoibhell, High Queen of Keltia. First serialised in the comic *2000 AD*, *Sláine: Treasures of Britain* (1997), written by Pat Mills and illustrated by Dermot Power, incorporates the Stone in a retelling of Arthurian mythology. Set after Arthur's defeat, when Britain has been over-run by Saxon warbands,

Sláine's task is to find the thirteen treasures of Britain, symbols of sovereignty that will awaken Arthur from his trance. These treasures include the Stone of Destiny (**colour plate 4**).

The appeal of 'alternative' or 'New Age' beliefs, emphasising spiritual values, mysticism and the natural world, has also generated modern myths about the Stone. Barbara Walker's *Woman's Dictionary of Symbols and Sacred Objects* (1988) provides a feminist perspective on the Stone:

> Much hostility was shown by patriarchal societies toward the ancient stone figures (or non-figures) that had been so long revered as maternal spirits. The famous Stone of Scone ... was once a Hag of Scone, that is, a Grandmother-Goddess, the same as the Cailleach, a queen of the elves or Elder Deities. Legend said she became a stone because she was cursed by a Christian missionary; but it seems likely that this Hag had always been a stone.

This and other modern myths rely on unattributed 'traditions' which are unconnected with the Stone's medieval mythology and have no historical basis.

Divergent versions of the myth appear in the earliest recorded traditions. Accelerating this process, modern myths exhibit an increasing tendency to depart radically from their medieval predecessors. This is apparent from the Stone's fictional portrayals and the appearance of myths appealing to increasingly narrow audiences, such as the British Israelites, Freemasons and Scottish Knights Templar. The contentious issue of the Stone's authenticity has generated its own genre of modern myths. The myth has mutated into a multiplicity of hybrid myths. The publicity surrounding the Stone's restoration in 1996 increased interest in the Stone, generating increasingly bizarre myths. One, posted on the world wide web, claimed that the Stone's return to Scotland precipitated the death of Diana, Princess of Wales. Although it is easy to dismiss such claims they are nevertheless important evidence of the Stone's continued relevance and the emergence of a new generation of myths.

The Stone of Destiny lies at the centre of an intricate web of myth and history and one that is still continuing to grow in size and complexity. In unravelling myth from history, the objective here has not been to discard the mythology that has accumulated around the Stone over the centuries. By tracing their evolution within a historical context, myths can be just as informative as historical sources and are integral to the Stone's significance and understanding.

3

THE STONE

The iron rings, the battered surface, the crack which has all but rent its solid mass asunder, bear witness to its long migrations.

Dean Arthur Stanley, *Historical Memorials of Westminster Abbey* (1868)

Regardless of its mythical origins, the Stone of Destiny's appearance and geology are central to determining its physical origins, function and authenticity. This chapter begins with a description of the Stone, including an analysis of its various features, their relative chronology and possible significance. This is followed by a history of the Stone's geological study and the implications of geology for identifying its place of origin. The chapter then assesses several earlier functions attributed to the Stone and concludes with a new interpretation of the Stone's original use and how it acquired its symbolic significance.

PHYSICAL APPEARANCE

The Stone of Destiny is unimpressive in appearance (**colour plate 5**). Even Mrs Rogers, who acclaimed the Stone as 'a priceless treasure', 'more precious than the priceless Koh-i-Noor', described it as 'this *"strange"* STONE, unsightly in outward form, unpretentious in outward shape, battered, scarred, and cracked – unhewn, unpolished and unrecognized'. It was, she claimed naïvely, 'so plain and unadorned that ... none should desire it; of size and weight sufficient to prevent [its] theft'.

The Stone is an oblong block, measuring $26\frac{3}{8}$ x $16\frac{1}{2}$ x $26\frac{3}{8}$ in (670 x 420 x 265mm), and weighing 336lb (152 kg). The Stone bears numerous signs of damage: its corners and lower edges are very uneven, having been badly chipped, while one corner has been broken away completely. The side which was exposed beneath the seat of the Coronation Chair exhibits most damage (**colour plate 6**). These scars represent the cumulative results of over 700 years' mistreatment. During that time, the Stone has suffered the attentions of visitors, antiquarians and geologists, has been removed from the Coronation Chair on several occasions and mistreated on at least one of these, as well as being damaged in a bomb attack.

The Stone has split into two fragments, probably along a naturally-occurring vertical flaw, detaching about a quarter of the Stone comprising an entire corner (**colour plate 7**). This is the 'crack' mentioned by the Dean of Westminster Abbey, Arthur Stanley,

8 *The Stone of Destiny, photographed* in situ *within the Coronation Chair after the removal of the seat sometime in the late nineteenth or early twentieth century*

in 1868. It is clearly visible on photographs in the Royal Commission's inventory of *Westminster Abbey* (1924) (**8**). But the Stone remained intact until 1950, when it was broken while being removed from Westminster Abbey by some Scottish students. The Stone was repaired in 1951 while still hidden in Scotland.

The role of human agency in shaping the Stone and altering its appearance over time is readily apparent. Its sides have been squared and roughly dressed with a chisel and punch, the marks of which are still visible on the Stone's rear face (**colour plate 8**). The use of different tools, the contrasting alignments of the tooling, and the varied quality of dressing indicates that it was executed by different hands, probably at different times.

A sequence is detectable in the features cut into the Stone's upper surface (**colour plate 7**). Although these are undated, a relative chronology may be constructed by identifying which features are earlier or later than others. The earliest is a rectangular panel, measuring 17 x 9in (430 x 230mm), which occupies the centre of the upper surface. This panel has been outlined with roughly chiselled grooves. The discontinuous nature of the groove on one side indicates that the panel was unfinished when work was abandoned. At one end, a second chiselled line attests a change in plan while it was being marked out. The inner groove is superimposed on the outer one, indicating that a slightly longer panel was originally intended.

The panel's function, and the reason why it was never completed, are unclear. It may have been intended to chisel out the area defined to create a recess or socket of uncertain function. Work may have been abandoned when it was realised that the Stone, weakened by the flaw, was in danger of splitting. Although it was often claimed that this panel held a metal plaque inscribed with the Stone's prophecy, this tradition originates in a sixteenth-century misinterpretation. Similarly, there is no evidence to support suggestions that the recess, once completed, was intended to house a cushion or holy relic.

The two iron rings attached to the Stone may have been added after the panel (**colour plates 5, 7, 9**). Each ring is suspended by an iron-link bar which is held by an iron staple. The staples are secured in two lead-filled sockets, one in the centre of each end of the Stone. The link bars enable the rings to be suspended above the Stone's upper surface, indicating that they were intended to facilitate the Stone's movement. As a result, the rings are usually attributed to the Stone's removal from Scone by Edward I in 1296, when it is widely believed that the Stone, suspended from a pole passed through the rings, was carried at shoulder height. But this is an impractical way of transporting the Stone; it is simply too heavy. A more realistic means of moving the Stone is by handbarrow (**colour plate 10**; **31, 68, 70**).

Moreover, there is no evidence to support the Stone's removal in 1296 as the historical context for the attachment of the rings. The Stone was moved on previous occasions. In 1249, the Stone was kept inside the abbey church at Scone but Alexander III was inaugurated on it in the open air, according to Fordun. The Stone was removed from the church for inauguration ceremonies and the rings *may* have assisted this.

When laid flat, the rings are accommodated within two recesses, roughly chiselled into the upper surface at both ends of the Stone (**colour plate 7; 8**). One recess is approximately rectangular, the other roughly circular in plan. These features have partially obliterated the grooves defining both ends of the rectangular panel, and therefore post-date this feature. As the recesses are specifically intended to house the rings, they were probably added at the same time as the rings. The rings, therefore, also post-date the panel.

The recesses save space by ensuring that the rings do not project above the Stone's surface. In another space-saving measure, the protruding ends of the iron staples securing the link bars to the Stone have been ground flat (**colour plate 9**). Together, these features would have enabled the Stone to be housed within a more confined space, both lower and narrower. A possible context for this is the Stone's accommodation within or beneath a throne, but whether this was a Scottish or an English throne is unclear. Although Edward I had the Coronation Chair constructed specifically to house the Stone, it is possible that the dimensions did not allow for the projecting staples and iron rings, necessitating the filing down of the former, and the creation of the recesses to hold the latter. This argument appears to be supported by the snugness with which the Stone fits beneath the seat of the Coronation Chair (**8**). However, the attribution of the rings and their recesses to the Stone's removal from Scone, and installation in the Coronation Chair, is inconsistent with another feature.

The other notable feature exhibited by the Stone's upper surface is its smoothness. Analysis by Peter Hill for Historic Scotland revealed that the surface was polished after the panel and the recesses were added. These features' rounded edges would have been sharper had they been cut through the Stone's smooth surface. This polishing may be the product of repeated walking on the Stone. But the uneven nature of its smoothed surface suggests that it was not level to begin with or that the Stone was subjected to repeated action such as kneeling or stepping over an extended period. Although this may seem inconsistent with the Stone's symbolic significance and its panel and rings, it suggests an alternative interpretation.

The Stone's upper surface is unlikely to have been polished after 1300, when the Stone was installed in the Coronation Chair in Westminster Abbey. The polishing is most likely to have occurred before the Stone left Scone and, therefore, while it was still the inauguration stone of the Scottish, or even Pictish, kings. This has implications for the dating of the other features. As the polishing post-dates the panel, the rings and their recesses, these must have been added *before* the Stone was removed from Scone in 1296. If the polishing resulted from repeated action on the Stone, the rings, recesses and panel must have been added *substantially* before 1296. With the possible exception of the filing down of the staples, the Stone's seizure by Edward I and its accommodation in the Coronation Chair appear to have left no identifiable traces. Unless, of course, this contributed to the Stone's battered appearance.

The only other features on the Stone's upper surface are two small, simple crosses; a Latin cross, crudely incised with a punch, in the centre of one edge and a Greek cross, incised with a sharper instrument, possibly a knife, in a corner (**colour plate 7**). The crosses' contrasting styles suggest that they were made by different hands. They were also made at different times. The rounded edges of the Latin cross indicate that it was carved before the Stone's surface was smoothed, while the more sharply defined edges of the Greek cross indicate that it was added after polishing. This cross, therefore, appears to be the latest in the sequence of features on the Stone's surface. Once again, however, only a relative chronology can be constructed; the dates of both crosses are unknown. Their significance is also unclear, but is presumably religious or symbolic. The crosses emphasise the Stone's religious associations and the ecclesiastical contexts in which it was kept from at least the mid-thirteenth century, at Scone and subsequently Westminster.

The addition of functional (the rings and recesses), unfinished (the grooved panel) and religious or symbolic (the crosses) features, as well as signs of wear (the smoothed surface), demonstrate that this is no ordinary stone. Moreover, the lengthy sequence of activity represented by these features attests that the Stone was used, and was therefore perceived to be significant, over a considerable period before 1296. The recesses and filed-down staples suggest that the Stone was kept in a confined space but that only its upper, polished surface was exposed. Although this may be consistent with its accommodation within a throne, another interpretation matches the evidence more closely. This will be discussed after looking at the Stone's geology and possible earlier functions.

GEOLOGY

Interest in the Stone of Destiny's geology began as early as the seventeenth century. In *Monumenta Westmonasteriensia* (1682), Henry Keepe recorded that 'it is of a blewish steel-like colour, mix'd with some eyes of red, triangular rather than any other form, and [on] being broken resembles a Peble'. Keepe drew no conclusions from this, but when Richard Pococke visited Scone in 1760 he rejected traditions of the Stone's Egyptian origin because it 'seems to be some of the Common Granite of Scotland'. Although he misidentified the rock, Pococke successfully recognised a means of determining the Stone's country, and possibly even place, of origin without having to rely on mythology.

Access to the Stone was facilitated by the disappearance of the quatrefoil wooden grille from the front of the Coronation Chair sometime between 1808 and 1818. The first recorded geological examination of the Stone took place in or before 1819, when Dr John MacCulloch described it as a calcareous sandstone. Despite complaining about the limitations of 'inspecting it in its present inclosed situation', E.W. Brayley gave a detailed analysis in *The History and Antiquities of the Abbey Church of St Peter, Westminster* (1823):

> It is a sandy granular Stone, a sort of debris of Sienite, chiefly quartz, with light and reddish coloured felspar, and also light and dark mica; with probably some dark green hornblende intermixed: some fragments of a reddish grey clay-slate, or schist, are likewise included in its composition: and, on the upper side, there is also a dark brownish-red coloured flinty pebble, which from its hardness has not been cut through, though immediately crossed by the indent.

Queen Victoria's coronation focused attention on the Stone and, in 1838, 'particles' of unspecified size and quantity were removed for comparative analysis, with the explicit intention of identifying the Stone's source. The technique used to collect these samples is unknown, but may account in part for the Stone's battered appearance and/or for some of the chisel marks.

From the 1860s, increased interest in the Stone stimulated its examination by the most distinguished Victorian geologists, as Frank Haes recalled:

> I was present, professionally, by the Dean's order ... on the day devoted to a geological examination of the structure of the stone by Professors Ramsay, Story-Maskelyne [Professor of Mineralogy at Oxford University and Keeper of Minerals in the British Museum] and others, as well as a goodly company of eminent architects, etc.

Sir Andrew Ramsay, Professor of Geology at University College London and Director General of the Geological Survey, described this occasion, in June 1865, when the Stone was removed from the Coronation Chair for inspection (**9**):

> The Coronation Stone consists of a dull reddish or purplish sandstone, with a few small embedded pebbles. One of these is of quartz, and two others of a dark material, the nature of which I was unable to ascertain. They may be Lydian stone. The rock is calcareous, and is of the kind that masons would call 'freestone' .... When the stone was placed on the table in the Abbey, the lower part of it was swept with a soft brush, and about as many grains of sand were thus detached from the stone as would cover a sixpence. Among these was a minute fragment of the stone itself. These were tested for me in Dr Percy's laboratory by Mr Ward, and found to be slightly calcareous. The red colouring-matter is peroxide of iron.

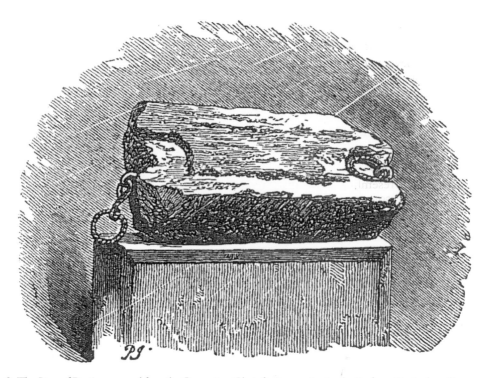

9 *The Stone of Destiny removed from the Coronation Chair for its examination by Professor Sir Andrew Ramsay and others in 1865. This engraving shows the Stone propped at an angle on a table or plinth, one of its iron rings and link bars suspended at its side. The rectangular panel on the Stone's upper surface is clearly visible.* From A.P. Stanley, *Historical Memorials of Westminster Abbey*, 1868

> There can be no doubt that the stone-dust brushed off the lower surface of the Stone truly represents the matter of which the mass is composed. It was simply loosened by old age; and when examined with the magnifying-glass, showed grains of quartz and a few small scales of mica, precisely similar to those observed in the Stone itself.

Although Ramsay did not describe his analysis, calcite was presumably indicated by effervescence when exposed to a dilute hydrochloric acid solution. However, a similar test in 1996 did not reveal the presence of calcite.

Sir Archibald Geikie, Director of the Geological Survey in Scotland, studied the Stone in April 1869. This was not his first analysis of the Stone, although nothing is known of his earlier examination(s); he may have been present with Ramsay in 1865. The Stone was also inspected in 1869 by the antiquarian John Stuart and again in, or shortly before, 1874 when it was incorrectly identified as limestone. In another examination, possibly by Sir J.J.H. Teall, 'minute fragments [were] obtained from the stone while it was being cleaned in 1892'.

There appears to have been little further analysis until George VI's coronation stimulated renewed interest in the Stone. In 1937, C.F. Davidson of the British Geological Survey conducted a microscopic analysis of the fragments obtained in 1892. F.J. Dimes, also of the Geological Survey, examined the Stone on its return to Westminster in 1951 to confirm that it was the same Stone taken by Scottish students. On the Stone's return to Scotland in 1996, the Secretary of State for Scotland, Michael Forsyth, stated that unspecified 'stringent tests' conducted in 1951 revealed the Stone's authenticity, but the results were never made public. And in 1996, minute samples from the Stone, which had been in Geological Survey collections since 1865 or 1892, were examined in thin section and compared petrographically with other samples of Old Red Sandstone from the Perth/ Dundee and Oban/Lorne areas.

Despite these various examinations, little progress was made in identifying the Stone's geological origin in the century after Pococke's comment. Instead, many found only confirmation of their preconceptions in the Stone's geology. Despite noting that 'it bears much resemblance to the Dun-stones, such are as brought from Dundee', only 18 miles (29km) east of Scone, Brayley attached more weight to mythology: 'Tradition intimates ... that this Stone was originally brought from Egypt, and it is remarkable that the substances composing it accord, in the grains, with the Sienite of Pliny, the same as Pompey's Pillar at Alexandria; but the particles are much smaller'. This was an enduring approach. W.J. Loftie claimed in *Westminster Abbey* (1890) that 'the Professor [Ramsay] is mistaken when he says there is no sandstone of the same character in Egypt, for one of the most celebrated statues in the world, the so-called *Vocal Memnon* [colossus of Amenhotep III], is made of it'. The Rev J.H. Allen asserted in 1902 that 'There is no rock of this kind in England, Ireland or Scotland .... [but] there is a stratum of sandstone near the Dead Sea just like this stone'. And Adam Rutherford commented in 1937 that 'The stone ... is dark purplish-red sandstone of the type found in southern Palestine'. Others were more cautious, but aware of the implications of the Stone's geology; Watson noted in 1910 that 'the geological evidence, if it does not actually disprove, at least does not support' the myth that the Stone was Jacob's Pillow.

After Pococke's analysis a century earlier, geology was not used to dismiss the Stone's mythical origins again until the 1860s. According to Ramsay:

> It is extremely improbable that the Stone has been derived from any of the rocks of
> the Hill of Tara .... Neither could it have been taken from the rocks of Iona .... That
> it belonged originally to the rocks round Bethel is equally unlikely ... and though
> we know of crystalline rocks ... in Egypt, I have never heard of any strata occurring
> there similar to the red sandstone of the Coronation Stone.

Geology also enabled the Stone's country of origin to be identified. According to Geikie, 'the stone is almost certainly of Scottish origin'. And despite referring to it as 'that ancient Irish monument', Dean Stanley asserted that 'there can be no question ... of its Scottish origin'. In 1937, Perkins admitted that 'the evidence of geology affords but little confirmation of its early wanderings. On the contrary, it tells very heavily indeed in favour of a Scottish origin'.

But even geologists were influenced by the Stone's mythology. MacCulloch observed in 1819 that the Stone is 'a calcareous sandstone, exactly resembling that which forms the doorway of Dunstaffnage castle', reiterating in 1824 that it was 'a fragment of a sandstone exactly similar to that of which Dunstaffnage Castle is built, and of which there is a tract along this coast. We could not indeed swear that it is a piece of the Oban sandstone, but it has every appearance of being nothing else'. Observing in 1868 that 'The country round Dunstaffnage ... consists of Old Red Sandstone, reddish or purplish in hue', Ramsay agreed that 'the doorway of Dunstaffnage Castle may have been derived from the same parent rock' as the Stone. Ramsay wrote to Geikie: 'I see according to your map Dunstaffnage stands on Old Red Sandstone. What is its colour and character there?'. Emphasising the difficulty of determining the Stone's colour, he now described it as 'reddish-grey sandstone'.

After the 1865 examination, according to Haes, 'The conclusion arrived at unanimously was that the stone was from the neighbourhood of Dunstaffnage'. Dean Stanley concurred: 'Its geological formation is that of the sandstone of the western coasts of Scotland .... thus far agreeing with the tradition of Dunstaffnage'. And Perkins claimed in 1937 that 'Pieces of hard red sandstone of this [the Stone's] description are frequently found in Scotland, not least in Argyllshire, where its authentic history begins'.

Although ostensibly based on geology, the identification of Dunstaffnage as the Stone's source rests solely on the myth that the Stone was kept at Dunstaffnage when it was first brought to Scotland. Geology and mythology were inextricably interlinked, but incompatible because the myth relates how the Stone was brought from Ireland *to* Dunstaffnage. Although the Stone and the masonry of Dunstaffnage Castle may comprise the same *type* of rock, they do not necessarily share the same source. The Stone's possible geological source is confined neither to Dunstaffnage, nor even to Argyll. A thick sequence of Devonian Old Red Sandstone, formed 370 million years ago, occurs in a belt running across Scotland from Argyll in the west to Tayside in the east. Both Scone and Dunstaffnage lie within this zone (**10**).

Indeed, Scone has long been identified as the Stone's possible source: 'Particles of the stone, detached in 1838, were compared with the quarries of Scone and thought to be identical', according to Dean Stanley. Despite preferring an Argyll source, Ramsay noted that 'The country around Scone is formed of Old Red Sandstone, and the tints of different portions of that formation are so various, that it is quite possible the Coronation Stone may have been derived from one of its strata'. Geikie's cautious conclusions were similar:

This afternoon I have again looked at the Coronation Stone. As I suspected, it really does not throw any certain light on its own history. So far as one can judge from the external surface, this block of sandstone may have been taken from almost any of the red sandstone districts of western or eastern Scotland. It cannot have come from Iona, I think, unless we suppose that it had previously been carried thither from the mainland – a supposition which its size and ordinary commonplace appearance seem to render unlikely. Nor does its character resemble that of the red sandstones of the north-west Highlands, while it is equally unlike the usual red sandstones of the south and south-east of Scotland. There are sandstones like it in the west of Argyleshire, and similar rocks abound in the southern half of Perthshire, in Forfarshire, and southward in the great Lowland valley. I do not see any evidence in

10 *Scotland, showing the occurrence of outcrops of Devonian Old Red Sandstone across the centre of the country, including around Dunstaffnage and Scone.* Redrawn after Fortey *et al.* 1997

> the stone itself why it may not have been taken from the neighbourhood of Scone; indeed, it perfectly resembles some of the sandstones of that district.

Geikie concluded that although 'the stone ... has been quarried out of one of the sandstone districts between the coast of Argyle and the mouths of the Tay and Forth ... there is no clue in the stone itself to fix precisely its original source'. It was impossible to trace the Stone's source with certainty.

A lively debate ensued, with those favouring the Stone's Biblical origin seizing on the geologists' uncertainty. J.B. Barnett vented his frustration thus:

> There is something remarkable in the nature of this stone evidently, for one geologist has declared that it is manifestly from the neighbourhood of Scone ... and was first heard of at Iona, so that that island must first have the honour of being its quarry. So here we have three quarries out of which to get this one stone! Did the three eminent architects [*sic*], assisted by three professors, examine the respective claims of Iona, Dunstaffnage and Scone when they all declared with such off-hand unanimity that it came from Dunstaffnage? Did they know anything at all about it?

The issue was even raised in the House of Commons after a complaint that the Stone's mythology had been omitted from a new notice beside the Stone. G. J. Shaw-Lefevre, the

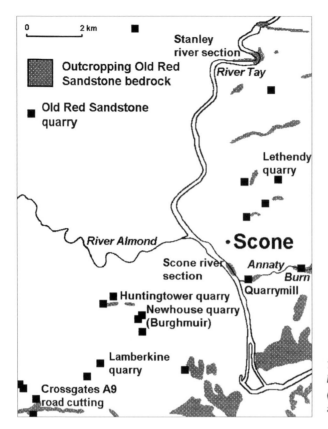

11 *The Scone area, showing the location of outcrops of bedrock and (mostly disused) quarries.* Redrawn after Fortey *et al.* 1997

Postmaster General and cabinet member, quoting Dean Bradley, replied on 12 May 1884 that: 'geologists have conclusively shown that the chair is of Scotch limestone, and that no stone of its kind is to be found in Palestine or Egypt'.

In 1937, Davidson compared microscopic fragments from the Stone with similar rocks from various locations and geological horizons. This confirmed the Stone to be a Lower Old Red Sandstone from Scotland. Moreover, several samples collected around Scone were 'petrographically indistinguishable' from the Stone. Microscopic analysis of a pea-sized pebble of porphyrite or andesite from the Stone provided an identical match with pebbles from Angus and Perthshire. Davidson concluded 'with reasonable certainty' that the Stone had been quarried in eastern Perthshire, probably close to Scone.

The geological evidence that the Stone originates within the Scone area is significant. Until 1296, the Stone's only known historical location was at Scone. In the absence of any evidence to the contrary, there is little reason to look further afield for the Stone's source: the Stone 'never was anywhere but at Scone', as Skene concluded in 1869. An origin in Perthshire rather than Argyll is also supported by what is probably the Stone's earliest recorded name, 'the Eastern Stone'. But despite the geological and historical evidence pointing to Scone, opinion remained divided about the Stone's source. A.W. Clapham noted in 1942 that 'the material is thought to be native to Argyll', while W. Douglas Simpson claimed in 1958 that 'the geological evidence is inconclusive – possibly with a slight, a very slight, bias in favour of Dunstaffnage'.

The comparative petrological examination conducted by the Geological Survey in 1996–97 was more comprehensive than any previously undertaken. This concluded that 'the Stone of Destiny is a block of Lower ORS from near Scone itself ... it may have originated from the Scone Formation at or near the old workings at Quarrymill', only 0.9 mile (1.4km) south-east of Scone (**11**). Moreover, the results were inconsistent with an Argyll source, while a Middle Eastern origin could be rejected. The Stone's origin may confidently be located within Scone's immediate vicinity.

EARLIER FUNCTIONS

The Stone of Destiny's role in royal inauguration rituals has been claimed to originate in its earlier function as a religious artefact. This is a modern manifestation of the Stone's origin myths, but emphasises functional origins. These claims reveal much about the development of the Stone's study and its modern myths, but are also relevant to the debate concerning the Stone's authenticity.

The perception of the Stone as a religious relic has influenced interpretations of its earlier functions and inspired theories of its saintly associations. Like Jacob's Pillow, several modern myths imbue the Stone with the sanctity derived from its association with a holy figure. This includes the Stone's identification as St Columba's Pillow. On his deathbed, Columba rested his head on a stone in his monastery on Iona, according to his *Lives* by the seventh-century abbots of Iona, Cummian and Adomnán. Adomnán described this as 'a stone which even today stands beside his burial-place as a kind of grave-pillar (*titulus monumenti*)'. The Vulgate Bible refers to sacred stones with similar phrases, describing the erection of Jacob's Pillow '*in titulum*', as a pillar or monument (Genesis 28:22).

The similarity between these phrases and Rishanger's identification of the Stone as Jacob's Pillow led Joseph Robertson in 1868 to claim that Jacob's and Columba's pillows were identical; Jacob dreamed of angels as he slept, while Columba had a vision of angels on his death bed. He then identified Columba's Pillow with the Stone because Kenneth mac Alpín translated Columba's relics from Iona to a church beside the River Tay. Robertson believed this was at Scone, where Columba's Pillow subsequently became the Stone. Skene demolished Robertson's claims, citing the absence of references to Jacob's Pillow in Scottish versions of the myth, the improbability that Kenneth would have removed Columba's gravestone from Iona, and that the church concerned was at Dunkeld, not Scone. The theory that the Stone originated as Columba's Pillow and gravestone does not stand up to scrutiny.

Archaeological and geological evidence also contradict Robertson's theory. Iona's many surviving early medieval memorial stones are of local material: Torridonian flagstones, mica-schists and granulites from Iona or the Ross of Mull. In contrast, the Stone is a block of Old Red Sandstone from the Scone area. It is most unlikely to have been an early medieval gravestone or to have had any historical connection with Iona or Columba. An early medieval grave marker, popularly known as 'St Columba's Pillow' (**12**), in the Abbey Museum on Iona has nothing to do with the Stone. Not only is its presence on the island inconsistent with the myth, but its association with Columba is ruled out by the form of

12 *'St Columba's Pillow', an eighth-century or later gravestone, found on Iona in the nineteenth century and now in the Abbey Museum, Iona.* Copyright: Royal Commission on the Ancient and Historical Monuments of Scotland

its incised ringed-cross, which dates to the eighth century or later; Columba died in 597.

Modern mythology associates other saints with the Stone. Pat Gerber implied a link with St Ninian by speculating that the Stone may have been a 'holy object' brought to Whithorn, St Ninian's foundation, by the earliest Scottish Christians. Gerber also pondered whether the original Stone is buried beneath the nave of Melrose Abbey. The Stone has also been interpreted as an early Christian altar stone. Skene suggested that it was 'the stone altar upon which Bonifacius first celebrated the Eucharist' after converting the Picts to the Roman liturgy in 710. St Boniface, or Curitan, was active amongst the northern Picts in the early eighth century and is associated with the possible see of Rosemarkie on the Black Isle. Andrew Lang's *History of Scotland from the Roman Occupation* (1900) claimed that 'This portable slab may have been ... an altar' used by Irish missionary saints. But there is no evidence to support any of these claims.

Nigel Tranter incorporated these interpretations in his fiction. In *The Stone* (1958), a character claims that Irish missionaries brought the Stone to Scotland and that 'it was probably originally a font, a baptismal basin. Possibly St Columba's own – which might partially account for its holiness'. In *The Steps to the Empty Throne* (1969), the Stone is 'the portable altar of a travelling saint, possibly Columba'. Archie McKerracher interpreted medieval accounts of the Stone as 'a precise description of a portable holy altar' and claimed that the great seals of Alexander I, David I and William depict the Stone as 'a plain, altar-like block'.

Portable altars were carried by some early medieval clerics, particularly missionaries practising in areas without churches. But the Stone is barely portable; it requires four able- bodied people to carry it, even then with difficulty (**colour plate 10**; **31, 70**). More realistically, the Stone may be a *mensa*, the upper slab of an altar. At the consecration of medieval churches, the altar stone's upper surface was engraved with five simple Greek crosses, one in the centre and four at the corners, symbolising the five wounds received by Christ at the crucifixion. The two crosses on the Stone are reminiscent of this, but the comparison is not close. Nevertheless, it is interesting to note Guisborough's statement that, in 1292, the Stone was kept close to the high altar in the abbey church at Scone.

A variation on this theme is that the Stone was a reworked Roman altar from a Roman military site; the fortress of Bertha lies across the River Tay from Scone. First suggested by James Richardson in 1951, this interpretation was developed in Tranter's *The Stone* (1958) and by Janet Christie in 1970. Christie claimed that medieval descriptions of the Stone are more consistent with the upper surface of some Roman altars than the Stone now in Edinburgh Castle. Moreover, the worship by the Celts of a Roman altar would explain the origins of the Stone's later significance, while the dedicatory inscription on a Roman altar might be the source of the Stone's prophecy.

Christie identified a broken altar from the Roman fort at Castlecary, Stirlingshire, as being of appropriate size and shape (**13**). But Roman altars are usually squared pillars, comprising a capital, shaft and base, and cannot be reconciled with medieval descriptions of the Stone as a hollowed marble chair. Some Roman altars are of comparable size to the Stone: a complete example from Castlecary measures 31 x 14 x 12in (785 x 350 x 310mm), although removal of its distinguishing features would make it smaller. Roman masonry

13 *The upper part of a second-century Roman altar from the Roman fort at Castlecary, Stirlingshire. The altar is dedicated to a goddess, but the inscription is incomplete.* The Hunterian Museum, University of Glasgow

was often reused in early-medieval western Europe, partly for utilitarian reasons but also because 'barbarian' ruling élites sought to draw on the legitimacy conferred by the Roman imperial past. Inscriptions were particularly evocative of such links and it is difficult to imagine why such features should have been removed to create a plain block.

A.W. Clapham claimed in 1942 that the Stone was originally a seat or cross base:

> On its upper surface are chip marks which probably indicate that the sides of the stone have at some time been cut down to the level of a central socket or recess represented by the present surface. If this raised part was present only at the sides and back, the result would be a rough seat not unlike the frith-stool at Hexham; if, on the other hand, all four sides were carried up the result would be a reasonable base-stone for a standing-cross.

But Clapham's theory rests on a misinterpretation of the panel on the Stone's upper surface.

Attempting to trace the Stone's significance further back in time, Lang speculated that 'an Irish missionary *may* have rescued for Christianity an earlier heathen sacred stone'. But the Stone's appearance led him to caution that: 'People who see in every sacred stone a grave-pillar which has developed into a fetish or a god, may observe that this example is an oblong block of red sandstone'.

There is no evidence that the Stone was reworked from an earlier artefact of any sort.

THE STONE REAPPRAISED

Of the Stone's possible earlier uses, the most plausible has received least attention. In 1865, Ramsay observed that 'It is a hewn stone, with chisel-marks on it, and looks like a stone originally prepared for building purposes', adding in 1868 that it 'had never been used'. The Stone certainly has the appearance of an ashlar, a large, square-cut block of masonry. Unused masonry carries a powerful Christian symbolism; Jesus is 'the stone rejected by the builders that became the keystone' (Mark 12:10; see also Acts 4: 11-12). Alternatively, the Stone may have come from a building. The absence of mortar need not be significant, as this could have worn off over time.

If the Stone was intended for, or derived from, a masonry building, it was probably a church. The earliest stone castles in Scotland date to the twelfth century but are few in number and none are recorded near Scone. In contrast, stone churches have a long history in this area. According to Bede's *Ecclesiastical History*, in 710 the Pictish king Nechtan son of Derelei successfully appealed to Ceolfrith, Abbott of Monkwearmouth-Jarrow in Northumbria, for builders to construct a church *more Romanorum*. The 'Roman style', of dressed and mortared masonry, contrasted with indigenous traditions of timber construction. The work of Ceolfrith's masons has been claimed to survive in the lower courses of the porch tower at Restenneth Priory, Angus, although this is now doubted (**14**).

14 *Restenneth Priory, Angus. Although the lower courses of the porch tower have been claimed to be the work of Northumbrian masons the Pictish king, Nechtan son of Derilei, requested from Ceolfrith, Abbot of Monkwearmouth-Jarrow, in 710, this masonry is probably later in date.* Copyright: Royal Commission on the Ancient and Historical Monuments of Scotland

Although there is no recorded physical evidence, there was almost certainly an early medieval church at Scone. Given the close links that existed between kingship and Church, Scone's description as a 'royal city' in 906 suggests the presence of a church, possibly associated with the Culdees and the forerunner of the priory founded there in 1114. The closest parallel to Scone as a Pictish and early Scottish royal centre is Forteviot, in Strathearn, only 6.8 miles (11km) south-west of Scone. Forteviot had a stone church, as a surviving ninth-century arch attests (**15**). The Stone may have been from, or intended for, a masonry church at Scone. This suggests a specific function, with both royal and ecclesiastical associations, which accounts for the Stone's form.

The Stone probably acquired its polished upper surface from being walked, stepped or knelt on over a prolonged period. If it was close to the high altar, as Guisborough states, its surface may have been worn smooth by the feet or knees of those celebrating mass. Other features are consistent with the Stone having been set in a floor. In marked contrast to its lower edges, the Stone's upper surface and sides are carefully dressed, enabling it to fit evenly and securely into a flagstone floor. Moreover, the recesses would have prevented worshippers from tripping over the rings. But why have rings at all? They must have been used to move the Stone and yet are unsuitable for carrying it any distance. But the rings are ideally suited for lifting the Stone out of a floor, as it would

15 *The sculptured stone arch, probably from a ninth-century royal church, found in the Water of May beneath Haly Hill at Forteviot, the site of a Pictish and early Scottish royal palace.* © The Trustees of the National Museums of Scotland 2000

have been impossible to grip otherwise. This also explains the Stone's slightly tapering form, enabling it to be inserted into, and extracted from, the floor more easily.

Why would the Stone have been set in the floor and raised frequently enough to require the rings? Although no kings are known to have been buried there, the abbey church at Scone contained royal tombs, including that of Matilda (Maud), queen of David I, who died in 1131. Earlier churches at Scone may also have housed royal tombs. Moreover, important early churches, particularly royal churches, often held the tomb of their founding saint and the relics of other saints. The presence of relics at Scone is supported by the presence nearby of an *annaid* placename, denoting an early church containing its founder's relics, the dedication of the abbey church to the Holy Trinity, and Scone's status, with Dundee, Melrose and Paisley, as one of 'the four heid pilgrimages of Scotland'. Those relics may have been used in rituals of royalty at Scone; a reliquary was presented to Alexander III at his inauguration in 1249. Such tombs and/or relics may have been kept in a crypt.

The Stone's form and the patterns of wear it exhibits are consistent with its function as a capping stone providing access to a sub-floor feature. That structure may have been some type of crypt. The Stone's location in 1292, close to the high altar, is consistent with that of the entrance to a crypt and Fordun's statement that, in 1249, the Stone was 'kept carefully in its own particular place' in the church at Scone; the Stone performed an important function at a specific location within the church. The Stone's weight would have deterred unauthorised access to these relics or their theft, a major concern throughout medieval Christendom.

Over time, the Stone may have acquired its sacred and symbolic significance from its close association with, and provision of access to, royal and/or saintly relics. The lifting of the Stone would have formed a necessary preliminary to any rituals involving those relics, perhaps including inauguration ceremonies. And, over time, the act of moving the Stone may have become an integral element of the ritual itself. Eventually, perhaps as a result of the destruction or theft of those relics, the Stone itself was invested with the reverence formerly attached to the relics themselves. That the Stone was revered as a holy relic by *c*.1060 is suggested by the reference in *The Birth of Áedán mac Gabráin* to someone swearing on 'the most powerful [or 'very famous'] Eastern Stone'. This transference of sacrality by association would explain why the Stone, despite its symbolism and royal associations, is not more impressive in appearance. The Stone was not originally significant and, even today, is not important for what it is. Instead, it was through its association(s) – direct or indirect, real or perceived – with early saints and/or kings, and the ritual(s) with which they or their relics were associated, that the Stone acquired its symbolism in its own right.

As a block of local sandstone, the Stone of Destiny has no intrinsic value. It is only as a result of the symbolic meaning invested in the Stone over time, and the historical associations it has acquired over the centuries, that it was – and still is – perceived to be so important in such varied contexts.

4

THE AUTHENTICITY
OF THE STONE

Whether we have the real stone or not is another question. John MacCulloch,
The Highlands and Western Isles of Scotland (1824)

Few issues concerning the Stone of Destiny have provoked as much controversy as its authenticity. Since 1781, many have claimed that the stone formerly kept in Westminster Abbey and returned to Scotland in 1996 is not the original Stone, upon which Scottish kings were inaugurated, but a fake. Did Edward I seize the 'real' Stone at Scone in 1296, or was he tricked into taking a substitute? Has a bogus stone featured in English and British royal coronations ever since? Or has the Stone been replaced at any other time?

These doubts have been expressed with increased vigour and frequency since 1950, when the Stone was removed from Westminster Abbey by Scottish nationalists. This episode not only rekindled the controversy surrounding the Stone's authenticity but also, it is claimed, provided an opportunity for substituting a fake stone, fuelling further suspicions. Was the same Stone returned the following year, or were the police and abbey authorities fooled by a fake? If the Stone removed in 1950 was not the genuine Stone and was replaced by another substitute, is the Stone now in Edinburgh Castle a 'double fake'? Uncertainties abound.

The cumulative effect of these persistent claims has been to create widely held and deeply seated doubts about the Stone's authenticity. Consequently, the Stone is now regarded with scepticism by many Scots, and by some as little more than a joke. Indeed, these suspicions are now so deeply engrained upon Scottish consciousness that they threaten to undermine the Stone's historical significance, investing it with new symbolism. The Stone's authenticity is fundamental to its role in royal coronation ceremonies, and its wider importance as a tourist attraction, an archaeological artefact, a subject of historical enquiry and, of course, a symbol of Scottish nationhood. The Stone's status, genuine or fake, demands analysis.

The Stone's authenticity has been challenged on several, unrelated grounds:

The Stone's appearance does not correspond with medieval descriptions and
   depictions of it
The Stone's size and geology are inconsistent with its use in royal inaugurations
The Scots fooled Edward I into taking a substitute stone in 1296 and hid the
   real Stone

The Scots never asked for the Stone's return after 1296

Scottish kings were still crowned on the Stone at Scone after 1296

The 'genuine' Stone still stands at Tara, in Ireland

The 'real' Stone was discovered on Dunsinane Hill in 1818

The original Stone was kept in Scotland after it was taken from Westminster Abbey
in 1950, and a fake returned instead

With the exception of the claims that the real Stone is still at Tara and that the Scots never asked for the Stone's return, which are discussed elsewhere, these arguments will be examined in turn before assessing the authenticity of the Stone now in Edinburgh Castle.

MEDIEVAL DESCRIPTIONS

Since 1781, the discrepancy between medieval descriptions of the Stone of Destiny and the stone then in Westminster Abbey has frequently prompted doubts about the latter's authenticity. Although medieval references are usually terse, several describe one or more aspects of the Stone's appearance: its form or shape, material, size, decoration and inscription.

From the earliest reference to the Stone, many English and Scottish medieval sources describe the Stone as a seat, chair or throne. In Edward I's warrant concerning John Balliol's inauguration in 1292 the Stone is the 'royal seat' (*regia sedes*). Similarly, it is the *sedile regium* in Bisset's *Processus* and appears in Langtoft's *Chronicle* as the 'Kinges sette'. Fordun refers to 'the stone, that is, the throne' (*lapidem ... scilicet, cathedram*) and describes how Alexander III was inaugurated 'upon the royal throne, that is, the stone' (*super cathedram regalem, scilicet, lapidem*; *in regali cathedra*). Walter Bower, Fordun's continuer, records that Alexander was inaugurated 'on this royal seat of stone' (*super hanc cathedram regalem lapideam*; *regali cathedra lapidea*). Wyntoun describes the Stone as the king's 'sege' and states that it was made 'for this kingis sete'. *La Piere d'Escoce* refers to 'the Stone ... on which the Kings of Scotland were placed in their seat' (*la piere ... Sur qei les Roys d'Escoce estoint mis en see*). Similarly, Rishanger mentions 'the stone which the Kings of Scotland were accustomed ... to use as a throne' (*lapide quo Reges Scotorum ... solebant uti pro throno*).

Although it is unclear from these sources whether the Stone was housed in a throne or comprised the throne itself, other descriptions are unambiguous. Fordun describes the Stone as 'a marble throne of very ancient workmanship, carved by a careful craftsman' (*marmoream cathedram, arte vetustissima diligenti sculptam opifice*), 'a block of marble cut in the shape of a throne' (*in formam cathedrae decisum ex marmore lapidem*) and 'the royal throne carved out of marble' (*cathedram marmoreo lapide decisam*). Guisborough records that the Stone was 'hollowed out ... [and] fashioned in the form of a round throne' (*concavus ... ad modum rotundae cathedrae confectus*). The late fourteenth-century *Chronicles of Melsa* qualify this: 'hollowed out and *partly* fashioned in the form of a round throne'.

The tradition of the Stone as a marble throne dominates medieval and later perceptions.

16 *The earliest illustration of the Stone of Destiny, portrayed as a throne of veined marble in this woodcut from Raphael Holinshed's* Chronicles *(1577). Instead of an accurate depiction of the real Stone, this conforms to mythological convention and portrays the Stone as it is described by medieval and later chroniclers*

This was the 'royal seat of marble' (*sedile regiae* [*regale*] *marmorium*) (Bisset), 'marble throne' (*cathedram marmoream*) and 'marble stone, fashioned like a chair' (*lapidem marmoreum, instar cathedrae compositum*) (John Mair, or Major), 'marble throne, or fatal stone as large as a seat' (*cathedram marmoream ... lapis cathedrae instar fatalis*) (Boece), 'chiar of merbill' (Bellenden) and 'chair of marbell stone' (Stewart). Indeed, so deeply-engrained was the concept of a *marble* throne that John Leslie consistently refers to the Stone simply as the 'marmor' or 'marmore'. English chroniclers followed Scottish conventions. The fifteenth-century additions to Robert of Gloucester's *Chronicle* specified it as a 'whyte marble Ston'. And, according to Holinshed, 'This stone was in fashion like a seate or Chayre', a 'chair of marble' and 'the marble stone' (**16**).

Few chroniclers diverged from these formulaic descriptions, although George Buchanan's *Rerum Scoticarum Historia* (1582) described the Stone as a 'marble rock' (*saxum marmoreum*) and a 'rough/unworked marble stone' (*lapidem marmoreum rudem*). Buchanan also distinguished between Stone and throne, describing how Kenneth mac Alpín had the stone 'enclosed in a throne of wood' (*in cathedram ligneum inclusum*). The Stone is described as a 'jewel' by Wyntoun ('gret iowell') and Blind Harry ('Iowell'), suggesting that it was believed to be of precious or ornate stone. Alternatively, this may reflect the Stone's perceived value or importance, as nineteenth- and twentieth-century parallels reflect: the Stone is referred to as an 'inestimable jewel' in George Chalmers' *Caledonia* (1807).

The Stone's size, when referred to, is invariably large. Listed as '*una petra magna*' in the Wardrobe Accounts of Edward I for 1298–99 and 1304, it is also a 'very large stone' (*lapis pergrandis*) (Guisborough), a 'gret iowell', a 'gret stane' (Wyntoun), and a 'mekill stane' (Stewart). Another notable feature was its inscription. Kenneth mac Alpín inscribed the prophecy's opening words, '*Ni fallat fatum*', on the Stone, according to Bellenden. Stewart also claimed that the Stone was gilded ('weill gilt with gold') and engraved with 'great letters of Greek' ('greit lettres of grew/Grauit'), presumably the prophecy or its first phrase.

There are marked discrepancies between these descriptions and the Stone now in Edinburgh Castle. The latter is neither of marble nor shaped like a chair, it bears no decoration or inscription and, although heavy, is not that large. As early as 1781, an unidentified antiquary, signing himself 'Antiquarius', cited differences between the Stone's described and actual appearance as evidence that this was not the original Stone. Scepticism about the Stone's authenticity spread. By 1807, Chalmers felt it necessary to assert that 'this stone, whatever doubts may have been entertained by some antiquaries, still remains in Westminster Abbey'.

Inconsistencies between the Stone and its medieval descriptions have been interpreted in three ways. 'Antiquarius' concluded that the genuine Stone was returned to the Scots during Edward II's reign (1307–27), and its place in the Coronation Chair filled by a substitute. But although its return was contemplated in 1328, the Stone remained at Westminster. Watson attempted to reconcile the Stone's present size with medieval accounts by claiming that the Stone was trimmed after it arrived at Westminster to enable it to be accommodated within the Coronation Chair. But Edward I's Wardrobe Accounts, which list the expenses incurred in the Chair's construction, do not record this. Moreover, as the Coronation Chair was made specifically to hold the Stone there should have been no need to alter it.

James Richardson highlighted anomalies between the sources and the Stone in an influential article in 1951. Developing these arguments and claiming that medieval descriptions are reliable, McKerracher claimed that the real Stone was 'plain, black, and marble-like, had metal hooks for carrying poles, and was hollowed on top like a font'. Similarly, Pat Gerber believed that the Stone 'was extremely large. It had some kind of shaping, with a concave top. It was carved in some way'. As these descriptions could not be equated with the rough block of flawed sandstone then in Westminster Abbey, they concluded that Edward could not have taken the genuine Stone from Scone. This argument has convinced many Scots.

Accounts of the Stone's origins reveal that mythology cannot be accepted at face value. This is equally true of mythical descriptions of the Stone as a marble throne. Chroniclers followed literary convention but embellished earlier accounts, describing the Stone as a grand and ornate marble throne. Other factors probably contributed to discrepancies between the Stone and its descriptions. Although the earliest sources belong to the period 1292–1306, the Stone's presence at Scone was beyond living memory for the later Scottish chroniclers. Unfamiliar with the Stone's appearance, chroniclers described what they considered to be a fitting royal inauguration stone or throne. English sources may have exaggerated the Stone's grandness to emphasise its significance as a war trophy.

In keeping with its symbolic significance, the Stone was described as grander in appearance and size than it was in reality. The formulaic descriptions of medieval chroniclers conformed to their expectations of what they believed the Stone *should* look like, basing their preconceptions on Continental and ecclesiastical parallels. Initially described as a seat, it later became a *cathedra* or bishop's throne. Befitting a bishop's status, a *cathedra* was perceived to be of richly carved stone or marble and great size. Moreover,

17 *The first great seal of Alexander III (1249–86)* W. de G. Birch, *History of Scottish Seals*

18 *The second great seal of Alexander III (1249–86), showing him in sitting in majesty on an ornate throne. Although it has been claimed that the Stone of Destiny was enclosed beneath the seat and behind a wooden latticework or iron grille, the Stone is not visible. Moreover, the seal is modelled on English prototypes and depicts a stylised and formulaic throne rather than a real one.* W. de G. Birch, *History of Scottish Seals*

the chroniclers were not using 'marble' in a specific sense, but as a generic label to describe a valuable stone. Medieval descriptions of the Stone as a marble throne cannot be accepted as accurate records of the Stone's appearance.

Some details in medieval sources have been attributed to misunderstandings rather than dismissed as products of the chroniclers' imaginations. Richardson and McKerracher suggested that Fordun's description of the Stone as 'sculptured in very antique workmanship' indicated that the Stone was enclosed within the throne behind a wooden lattice or iron grille, the shadows it cast giving the Stone the appearance of being ornately carved. They claimed that this may relate to the Scottish throne before 1296 and that such an arrangement is depicted on the seals of Alexander III (**17, 18**). Alternatively, this reflects an enduring confusion between the stone and the ornately carved wooden throne that presumably held it. Boece's statement that the prophecy's first words were inscribed on the Stone may be attributed to a misinterpretation of *Liber Extravagans*, which refers to the prophecy 'attached' to the Stone, meaning simply that it was *associated* with the Stone. Mistakenly assuming that the prophecy was *physically* attached, and embellishing earlier accounts, Boece described it as *inscribed on* the Stone.

19 *The great seal of Edgar (1097–1107), depicting the king wearing a lily crown and sitting on an X-framed throne-stool with animal-headed terminals and clawed feet.* W. de G. Birch, *History of Scottish Seals*

Discrepancies between the Stone and its medieval descriptions may be attributed to several factors, including a lack of first-hand knowledge of the Stone and a confusion between the Stone and the throne that may have held it. Moreover, awareness that Scottish kings were inaugurated on the Stone probably encouraged the assumption that it was a seat or throne. As medieval chroniclers relied extensively on earlier sources, this soon resulted in them adopting a stereotyped description of the Stone as a marble chair. Their literal acceptance resulted in these descriptions dominating perceptions of the Stone for several centuries. The Stone was identified so closely with the Scottish throne that the two were perceived to be synonymous. The enduring nature of this confusion is apparent in some nineteenth-century names, such as the 'Royal Chair of Stone'.

The interpretation of the Stone as a throne has re-emerged recently. McKerracher and Gerber both employed medieval descriptions of the Stone without distinguishing between historical fact and mythological embellishment. Accepting these sources at face value leads inevitably to the conclusion that the Stone which Edward removed from Scone is a fake. But, like the origin myths in which many appear, these accounts cannot be accepted literally. Formulaic and mythological descriptions of the Stone as a marble throne are unreliable and do not apply to the genuine Stone. Medieval descriptions are irrelevant to the Stone's authenticity.

MEDIEVAL DEPICTIONS?

The Great Seals of Scotland were supreme symbols of the royal authority carried by the laws and charters to which they were attached. Impressed in beeswax on both sides, their obverse depicts the king in majesty, seated on his throne with the symbols of kingship, while the reverse portrays him on horseback as a warrior king. These seals, it has been claimed, record the appearance of the Scottish throne before 1296 and, therefore, are relevant to the debate concerning the Stone's authenticity.

20 *The great seal of Alexander I (1107–24)*
W. de G. Birch, *History of Scottish Seals*

21 *The great seal of Alexander II (1214–49)*
W. de G. Birch, *History of Scottish Seals*

In 1951, Dr James Richardson examined the seals for evidence of the Stone's authenticity. Richardson noted that the box-like seat of the throne – which, he assumed, encased the Stone – was the height of a chair, enabling a king to sit normally. In contrast, the seat of the Coronation Chair in Westminster Abbey had to be raised on a step with carved lions to make it of sufficient height (**colour plate 11**). Richardson concluded that the original Stone was considerably thicker than that removed by Edward I and that the stone presented to Westminster Abbey was therefore a fake.

Developing Richardson's ideas, McKerracher argued that the seals prove that the Stone was housed within the Scottish throne until 1296. McKerracher claimed that three forms of throne are represented on the seals. The earliest, on the seal of Edgar (1097–1107) (**19**), is unlikely to have encased the Stone. But the seals of Alexander I (1107–24), David I (1124–53), Malcolm IV ('the Maiden', 1153–65), William ('the Lion', 1165–1214), and Alexander II (1214–49), allegedly depict the Stone as a 'plain, altar-like block resting on the floor', forming a seat within a central recess in the throne (**20-22**). Alexander's and David's seals, McKerracher added, 'show quite clearly that the block has metal carrying hooks, top and bottom, on all four corners ... held by perforated metal bands running round the stone'. This arrangement, he claimed, is consistent with the more reliable medieval descriptions of the throne. But, emphasising the stylised nature of royal seals and weakening McKerracher's argument, English great seals exhibit a similar feature.

The later seals, McKerracher maintained, show the Stone beneath the throne's seat. On the surviving fragment of Alexander III's (1249–86) early seal, the Stone is enclosed by a latticework grille and on his later seal it is behind a grille, below an ornate throne (**17, 18**). Finally, on the seal of John Balliol (1292–1304) the Stone is completely encased within a higher throne, necessitating the king's use of a footstool and cushion (**23**).

22 *The great seal of William 'the Lion' (1165–1214)*
W. de G. Birch, *History of Scottish Seals*

23 *The great seal of John Balliol (1292–96)*
W. de G. Birch, *History of Scottish Seals*

The problem with these ingenious arguments is that they rest solely on the evidence of the seals; the thrones themselves have not survived. And, as symbols of royal authority, an element of exaggeration or artistic licence might be expected in these images. More fundamentally, Scottish seals were modelled closely on English exemplars so that the thrones portrayed are formulaic in style. These cannot be accepted as reliable representations of Scottish thrones. Moreover, it is impossible to distinguish between the Stone and the thrones allegedly housing it. The Stone is not identifiable on a single seal. The great seals of the Scottish kings are therefore irrelevant to the debate concerning the Stone's authenticity.

MODERN ASSUMPTIONS

Most claims that the Stone removed from Scone by Edward I was a fake are based not on historical evidence, but modern assumptions concerning the appearance, material and size of the 'genuine' Stone of Destiny. These preconceptions feature prominently in the debate surrounding the Stone's authenticity.

A common assumption is that the Stone now in Edinburgh Castle is incompatible with its role in royal inauguration rituals. For example, Gerber claimed that:

> If the Stone of Destiny did originate in the Holy Land ... it may well be composed of meteorite. If it came from Ireland or Iona, marble is the most likely material. Alternatively it may be basalt, black and polished with age. Least likely of all is sandstone, the material of the Stone Edward I took to Westminster.

Moreover, this Stone is not only sandstone, but is also flawed.

The tradition that the 'real' Stone is a meteorite first appeared in 1819 in a letter reporting the discovery of a large stone 'of the meteoric or semi-metallic kind'. This, allegedly, was the original Stone. Its meteoric origin is a key element in the Stone's modern mythology and is supported by claims that meteorites are sacred to many religions. In Nigel Tranter's *The Stone* (1958), a character describes the 'real' Stone as 'one of the plutonic stones – heat fused . . . Iron hard. That's the stuff of meteorites .... many of these ancient relics *were* made out of meteorites – the ancients considered them very holy, having come down from heaven'. The parallel cited is invariably the Black Stone in the Ka'aba at Mecca, Islam's holiest shrine. But little significance was attached to these claims during the nineteenth century; MacCulloch simply observed that 'It does not follow ... that because there is a black stone at Mecca, there must have been one at Dunstaffnage'.

Other modern assumptions concern the Stone's height or thickness. In contrast to the Stone now on display, which is only 10⅜in (265mm) thick, Richardson and McKerracher claimed that the 'genuine' Stone must have been at least 18-20in (457-508mm) high. Gerber expressed this case more colourfully:

> Eleven inches is the height of a decent-sized Victorian chamber pot. Any monarch sitting on a stone of such meagre dimensions would have looked utterly ridiculous – even the knees of a relatively small man would have been up around his ears. Try it. Would you crown a king, who was supposed to look heroic and dignified, on such a thing?

Indeed, some Scots believe the present Stone to have been better suited as a cess pit cover, the 'Cludgie Stane', than for the inauguration of kings, although how it could have functioned as such is conveniently ignored. But if the Stone was held in a throne its height is irrelevant.

Tranter's *The Stone* describes the 'real' Stone as:

> a great squared block, with an uppermost face roughly 28 inches long by 20 inches wide ... an oblong face, with the lateral ends curved over into something like carved

24 *The late Nigel Tranter believed the 'genuine' Stone of Destiny might look like this. His design incorporates an unlikely combination of Pictish keywork, Celtic interlace and zigzags.* Nigel Tranter, *Nigel Tranter's Scotland*, 1981

rolls – volutes ... and the centre hollowed out into the likeness of a shallow wide bowl, in smooth flowing lines. The stone itself was dark, almost black-seeming ... and non-granular, feeling hard, almost glazed to the touch.

It was also decorated in 'typically Celtic workmanship' (**24**):

All four sides of the Stone were differently carved with intricate and comprehensive designs of broad-ribbon interlacing, diagonal key patterns, and elaborate spirals culminating in raised bosses, within borders of a kind of dog-tooth tracery ... called herringbone. Only the upper surface was plain, save for the basin-shaped depression and the volutes at the ends ... it was ... about eighteen inches high, darkly vigorous in concept, well proportioned, solid yet of graceful lines.

Tranter's description of the Stone as an impressive object of artistic merit that remained hidden in Scotland, in contrast to the plain sandstone block then in Westminster Abbey, appealed to Scottish popular opinion and influenced subsequent debate on the Stone.

Gerber's reconstruction of the 'real' Stone assumed that 'It is almost beyond doubt that such a revered object ... would not only have been elaborately carved, but also painted' and that 'there are few reasons to think it would be anything other than a most beautifully decorated artefact'. But the only justification cited is the rich artistic tradition of early-medieval Britain and that 'Celtic peoples have always loved bright colours'. Combining medieval descriptions, the thrones depicted on seals and the Dunadd footprint with features derived from Roman altars and Pictish sculpture, Gerber claimed that:

the Stone we are looking for stands at least 17 inches high, 18 inches deep and 32 inches wide. It is dark, polished and painted, with some spirals, [and] a hollow in the top not unlike a footprint. There will be traces of carved lettering probably in

Latin, possibly in Gaelic, once picked out in red and white or into which precious metal has been run. There may be several other carvings, such as the Irish Harp, a Pictish Boar, [or] Daniel and his lions. It has legs or feet like eagle's claws and, running up and down the front edges, the legs of animals, possibly lizards. On either side pairs of crook-shaped hooks were fixed so that it could be slung on two poles for transport.

Gerber added that 'The Stone might have a Cross on it, and also spirals – for sun-worship'. This description of ill-assorted elements may be dismissed as complete speculation.

There is no inherent reason why Scottish kings should not have been inaugurated on a block of sandstone. After all, successive English and British monarchs have been crowned on this very Stone. If it was – and indeed still is – good enough for them, why should Scottish kings not have been installed on it? More fundamentally, its form and appearance are irrelevant because the Stone is not of value in its own right. Instead, the Stone's importance is derived from its symbolic associations and the meaning invested in it.

EDWARD I AND THE 'SUBSTITUTE STONE'

A persistent tradition maintains that Edward I did not remove the real Stone of Destiny but a substitute. This was first claimed in 1819 and appeared to be supported by growing geological evidence that the Stone originated in the Scone area. This tradition is now one of the mostly deeply-seated modern myths surrounding the Stone, again probably because of its popularisation in historical fiction. A character in Tranter's *The Stone* describes how:

> the Stone which Edward Plantagenet stole from Scone Abbey ... and took away south with him, the Stone he thought was the Stone of Destiny, was just a plain unworked block of Old Red Sandstone, dug out of a quarry at Scone specially for him ... the real Stone ... much bigger, richly carved, and saddle-shaped, was buried somewhere near the Abbey and two years later dug up, brought across the Tay, and hidden again ... for safer keeping .... It wasn't to be expected ... that the custodians of the Stone of Destiny, Scotland's most precious relic, would not have sought to keep it from Edward, in the War of Independence? After all, they knew he was coming for it. They had plenty of warning. So they fooled him with this other stone.

Tranter's *The Steps to the Empty Throne* (1969) describes the hiding of the Stone and its reappearance at the coronation of Robert I at Scone in 1306. Abbot Henry of Scone tells Robert how he fooled Edward into taking a sandstone block obtained from a local quarry while the real Stone was hidden in a cave on Moncreiffe Hill, 4.3 miles (7km) south of Scone. Tranter raised another possibility in *The Stone*. Frustrated by the Scots, who had hidden the Stone, Edward himself found a substitute and returned in triumph to London, where no-one was any the wiser, with what he claimed was the genuine Stone.

Like Tranter's description of the Stone, his retelling of the myth that Edward was tricked into taking a fake stone has had a profound influence. McKerracher claimed:

> There can be little doubt Edward had been duped. The monks of Scone Abbey had fully six weeks' warning of Edward's approach. As only a few people knew what the real Stone looked like, enclosed as it was within the throne, it was a simple matter to substitute a flawed building block from a nearby quarry ... The real stone was almost certainly hidden by Abbot Henry.

These speculative interpretations are heavily reliant upon assumptions concerning the English raid on Scone: that the monks had sufficient warning of the English advance; that they were aware, or suspicious of, Edward's intentions; that they intended to hide the Stone and had the means, including sufficient time and manpower and an adequate hiding place to achieve this. There is no evidence to support any of this. The principal assumption rests ultimately on modern values and patriotic emotions: surely the Scots would not have been careless enough to allow the stone on which their kings were inaugurated to fall into English hands? The nature of Edward's campaign suggests otherwise. That Edward was fooled into taking a stone substituted for the genuine Stone represents modern Scottish wishful thinking rather than historical fact. Indeed, Edward was unlikely to have been fooled because two of his closest associates, Anthony Bek, Bishop of Durham, and John de St John, had probably seen the Stone when they installed John Balliol at Scone in 1292.

Another argument used to support the claim that Edward did not remove the real Stone is that Scottish kings were still inaugurated on it *after* 1296. This confusion has a long history. As early as 1582, Buchanan mistakenly claimed that Robert was the last Scottish king to be crowned on the Stone. According to Fordun, Bruce was crowned 'on the royal seat' (*in sede ... regali*) at Scone, but there is no reference to a stone in this or any other account. It is unclear if the throne, which was probably of wood, formerly held the Stone or was a replacement post-dating 1296. Similarities between the throne depicted on Robert's first seal and those on earlier seals are irrelevant because of the seals' stereotyped portrayal of thrones. Indeed, Robert's second seal is closely modelled on French prototypes (**25**).

Conceding there is no evidence that Robert was crowned on the Stone, McKerracher claimed that Abbot Henry must have decided to leave the Stone in hiding because of the risk that Edward would return to seize it. But Robert's contested kingship and his coronation when much of Scotland was under English occupation strongly suggest that, had the Stone been available, it would have been used and that medieval chroniclers would have recorded this.

Sealing the argument, there are also reliable historical records of the Stone's presentation to Westminster Abbey. By 1306, the Stone was no longer at Scone, having been seized by Edward a decade earlier. For this we are dependent not solely on English sources; the Scots soon complained of its seizure, as Bisset's *Processus* attests, and medieval Scottish chroniclers are also consistent in their accounts of the Stone's removal. But despite its mythical nature and modern origins, the tradition that Edward was deceived by an ordinary, quarried slab, substituted for the genuine Stone, is still believed by many Scots.

25 *The second great seal of Robert I (1307–29). The throne reverts to an X-framed stool, with bird-headed terminals and clawed feet, but the seal is modelled on French prototypes.* W. de G. Birch, History of Scottish Seals

THE 'DUNSINANE STONE'

The 'substitute Stone' is linked with another modern myth. If Edward *was* tricked, what happened to the original Stone of Destiny? The myth conveniently explains the Stone's subsequent disappearance; by the time the Stone was safe from the English, the few monks who knew its hiding place were dead.

The real Stone, it is claimed, was rediscovered in an underground chamber on Dunsinane (or Dunsinnan) Hill, 3 miles (5km) east of Scone, in 1818. An unsigned letter titled 'Macbeth's Castle (Curious Discovery)' in the *Times* on 1 January 1819 reported that:

> On the 19th Nov, as the servants belonging to the West Mains of Dunsinane house were employed in carrying away stones from the excavation made among the ruins that point out the site of Macbeth's castle here, part of the ground they stood on suddenly gave way, and sunk down about six feet, discovering a regularly built vault, about six feet long and four wide. None of the men being injured, curiosity induced them to clear out the subterranean recess, when they discovered among the ruins a large stone, weighing about 500 lb, which is pronounced to be of the meteoric or semi-metallic kind. This stone must have lain here during the long series of ages since Macbeth's reign.
>
> Beside it were also found two round tablets, of a composition resembling bronze. On one of these two lines are engraved, which a gentleman has thus deciphered – 'The sconce (or shadow) of kingdom come, until sylphs in air carry me again to Bethel'. These plates exhibit the figures of targets for the arms. From time immemorial it has been believed among us here, that unseen hands brought Jacob's pillow from Bethel, and dropped it on the site where the palace

of Scoon now stands. A strong belief is also entertained by many in this part of the country, that it was only a representation of this Jacob's pillow that Edward sent to Westminster, the sacred stone not having been found by him. The curious here, aware of such traditions, and who have viewed these venerable remains of antiquity, agree that Macbeth may, or rather must, have deposited the stone in question at the bottom of his castle, on the hill of Dunsinane (from the trouble of the times), where it has been found by the workmen.

The same letter appeared in several English and Scottish newspapers over the following month.

A similar account appeared in Seton Gordon's *Highways and Byways in the Central Highlands* (1948):

> ... somewhere around the dates 1795–1820, a farm lad had been wandering with a friend on Dunsinnan ... soon after a violent storm. The torrential rain had caused a small landslide, and as the result of this a fissure, which seemed to penetrate deep into the hillside, was visible. The two men procured some form of light and explored the fissure. They came at last to the broken wall of a subterranean chamber. In one corner of the chamber was a stair which was blocked with debris, and in the centre of the chamber they saw a slab of stone covered with hieroglyphics and supported by four short stone 'legs'. As there was no evidence of 'treasure' in the subterranean apartment the two men did not realise the importance of their 'find' and did not talk of what they had seen.
>
> Some years later one of the men first heard the local tradition, that on the approach of King Edward I the monks of Scone hurriedly removed the Stone of Destiny to a place of safe concealment and took from the Annety Burn a stone of similar size and shape, which the English king carried off in triumph. When he heard this legend, the man hurried back to Dunsinnan Hill, but whether his memory was at fault regarding the site of the landslide, or whether the passage of time, or a fresh slide of earth, had obliterated the cavity, the fact remains that he was unable to locate the opening in the hillside.

Gordon's account appears to have been derived from the letter of 1819, its vagueness about the date of the discovery and absence of detail pointing to a dimly remembered tale that had passed into local folklore. These accounts, therefore, are not independent and do not corroborate each other.

The letter's author was not reporting events at first hand and was no historian. Macbeth (1040–57) cannot have hidden the Stone in 1296. Attempting to resolve this discrepancy, Robert Chambers' *The Picture of Scotland* (1827) claimed that:

> Macbeth, from an implicit faith in the sacred character of the stone, and that the possession of it would insure the continuance of his sovereignty, transferred it to a close concealment in his fortress, substituting in its place a similar stone, which has ever since been accepted as the real one.

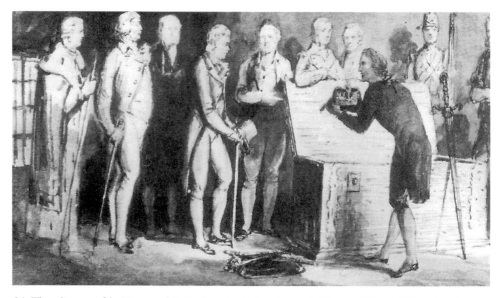

26 *The rediscovery of the Honours of Scotland, the Scottish regalia, on 4 February 1818. Sir Walter Scott is shown with his arms resting on the chest's raised lid. The Honours of Scotland had been locked in the oak chest in the Crown Room of Edinburgh Castle since the Union of the Parliaments, when Scotland lost its own parliament, in 1707*

This is simply a variant of the 'substitute Stone' myth.

The vague descriptions of items allegedly discovered with the stone also arouse suspicion. But McKerracher was convinced that the 'Dunsinane Stone' was the 'real' Stone, while Gerber also accepted these sources as reliable. Believing that it was the origin of the prophecy, McKerracher attempted unconvincingly to make sense of the enigmatic inscription on one of the 'round tablets' by translating it into Gaelic and retranslating it as 'Under your protective shadow lies the kingdom until angels carry you back to Bethel'. This simply reflects the Stone's mythical origin as Jacob's Pillow and Jacob's dream in the Book of Genesis.

Suspicions are heightened by the complete absence of any corroboratory evidence of the discovery; there are no independent accounts or surviving artefacts. This seems remarkable given the unusual nature of the finds and high levels of interest in both the Stone and Dunsinane. According to the letter, 'This curious stone has been shipped for London for the inspection of the scientific amateur, in order to discover its real quality'. The stone's claimed weight suggests that it would have been difficult to misplace, while its allegedly meteoric origin would have distinguished it from more mundane rocks. Despite this, the stone and 'round tablets' have disappeared without trace.

The inescapable conclusion is that the 'Dunsinane Stone' never existed beyond the imagination of its perpetrator and the popular tradition that his letter inspired. The 'Dunsinane Stone' links subjects of contemporary antiquarian interest. Exploiting existing doubts about the Stone's authenticity and Dunsinane's traditional association with Macbeth, the hoax located the alleged discovery on the hill, adding Macbeth's role

27 *The Honours of Scotland, as displayed in the Crown Room of Edinburgh Castle shortly after their discovery*

in substituting the original Stone. But the discovery was largely ignored or dismissed, as MacCulloch did:

> Some one has lately amused himself with supposing that the original stone was a meteorolite ... which was concealed at Dunsinnan, and that this [the Stone then in Westminster Abbey] was substituted in its place. When we are at the trouble of supposing, we may as well suppose any thing; or admit, which is much better, that it was really Jacob's pillow.

The 'Dunsinane Stone' was a product of its age. The early nineteenth century saw an increased interest in Scotland's past and a reawakening of Scottish national identity; this followed decades of apathy and neglect after the Treaty of Union of 1707, under which the Scots lost their own parliament. Sir Walter Scott played a prominent role in this revival, and not only through his historical novels. Scott persuaded the Prince Regent, the future George IV, to allow him to search for the Honours of Scotland, the Scottish crown jewels, which had been kept under lock and key in Edinburgh Castle since 1707. Scott's rediscovery of the regalia (**26**), in February 1818, was widely celebrated in Scotland and sparked a renewed sense of national pride. This reached its climax in George IV's state visit to Scotland in 1822, an event which Scott himself organised. Scotland was gripped by romantic nationalism. The Honours were publicly displayed from 26 May 1819 (**27**). The alleged discovery of the 'Dunsinane Stone' less than six months after rediscovery of the Honours was no coincidence. These events and the accompanying publicity probably inspired the hoax that the Stone, a more

28 *The multiple-ramparted citadel on the summit of Dunsinane Hill, Perthshire, from the air. Traditionally reputed to be the ruins of Macbeth's castle, the site attracted the attentions of early antiquarians and was the scene of several excavations between c. 1790 and 1856, resulting in the disturbed ground at the eastern end of the interior.* Copyright: Royal Commission on the Ancient and Historical Monuments of Scotland

29 *Plan of the excavated citadel on Dunsinane Hill, 1854, also showing the trenches from James Playfair's excavation in the 1790s. The location of the underground chambers is indicated and, within one, the findspot of the quernstone.* Copyright: Royal Commission on the Ancient and Historical Monuments of Scotland

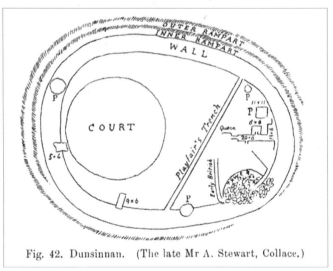

Fig. 42. Dunsinnan. (The late Mr A. Stewart, Collace.)

ancient and arguably potent symbol of Scottish nationhood, had not been removed but remained hidden in Scotland.

In addition, the fortifications on Dunsinane Hill attracted considerable antiquarian interest from the 1770s (**28**). 'Macbeth's Castle', as it was traditionally known, was the scene of intermittent excavations from the 1790s (**29**) and the letter refers to an 'excavation'. Moreover, the subterranean vault mentioned may be one of two chambers recorded in 1854 (**30**), possibly souterrains for the storage of foodstuffs. One was

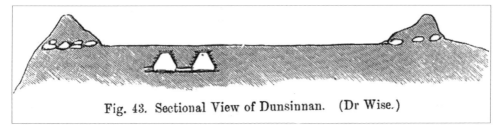

Fig. 43. Sectional View of Dunsinnan. (Dr Wise.)

30 *Section of the citadel on Dunsinane Hill, showing the twin subterranean chambers within the interior.* Copyright: Royal Commission on the Ancient and Historical Monuments of Scotland

reported to have contained a quernstone for grinding grain and, if known about earlier, this could have inspired the hoax.

The 'Dunsinane Stone' was forgotten during the nineteenth century, while the historical and geological study of the Stone flourished, only to gain acceptance during the twentieth century. In 1968, Wendy Wood, a tireless campaigner for the Stone's restoration to Scotland, slipped a message through the railings surrounding the Coronation Chair in Westminster Abbey. It declared: 'This is not the original Stone of Destiny. The real Stone is of black basalt marked with hieroglyphs and is inside a hill in Scotland'. This hoax has successfully fooled several recent writers on the Stone. Indeed, as a result of Archie McKerracher's articles, more credence is now attached to the 'Dunsinane Stone' than at any other time since its alleged discovery. However, neither is the 'Dunsinane Stone' the genuine Stone, nor is there any evidence to indicate that a stone was ever found on Dunsinane Hill. This 'tradition' rests on a hoax and has no bearing on the Stone's authenticity.

MODERN FAKES AND HOAXES

Hoaxes concerning the Stone of Destiny's authenticity are not confined to the nineteenth century. In 1959, 'C. Iain Alasdair Macdonald' claimed in several letters to be its hereditary custodian and to know the Stone's hiding place on the Isle of Skye. He gave the following description:

'The Stone' which measures approx 11 inches by 21 inches is supposed to be resting in its origional [sic] seating of marble but presume half of it is missing. The Stone as far as I can make out resembles a well filled pillow and has many weird superstitions.

Another letter purported to quote from a document dated 1720 which was allegedly found in 'an antique chest' hidden with the stone.

These poorly-written, long and rambling letters omit details and key information, including, predictably, the stone's location. Attempts to identify and trace the author proved fruitless. There is no evidence to link the Stone with Skye or the MacDonalds, while Clan MacDonald maintains that it has no knowledge of the 'Skye Stone'. The vague references to a marble seat, pillow and 'weird superstitions' reveal an elementary knowledge of the Stone's mythology. The letters also contain factual errors about the MacDonalds of the Isles, while references to the 'Stone of Destiny' are inconsistent with a document of 1720. This document allegedly claimed that the Stone was moved to Skye in 1329. As this is 33 years after the Stone was removed from Scone, Edward must have been duped, while the original Stone remained in Scotland. The 'Skye Stone' is another manifestation of the 'substitute Stone' and must be dismissed as a hoax.

Like the 'Dunsinane Stone', the 'Skye Stone' was a product of its age. The removal of the Stone from Westminster Abbey in 1950, its return in 1951 and the coronation of Queen Elizabeth in 1953 generated much publicity and reopened the debate concerning the Stone's authenticity. These events probably inspired the hoax.

These letters initiated the popular tradition that the Stone is hidden in a cave behind a waterfall on Skye. Once again, Nigel Tranter's historical fiction helped to disseminate this myth. *The Path of the Hero King* (1970) relates how Robert I made Angus Og of the Isles the dewar, or hereditary keeper, of the Stone, instructing him to keep it safe on an island after Robert's son was crowned. A version of this tradition also featured in a 1997 episode of the BBC Scotland comedy drama, *Hamish MacBeth*. The 'Skye Stone' illustrates not only the constantly evolving nature of the Stone's mythology, but also how myths concerning the Stone's authenticity have proliferated, diversified and taken root within Scottish popular folklore since the 1950s.

The taking of the Stone in 1950–51 was a key event in shaping popular opinion about the Stone. As well as stimulating increased interest, the Stone's illicit removal also revived doubts about its authenticity. In February 1951, James Richardson claimed that the Stone removed from Westminster Abbey was not the genuine Stone and that Edward had seized a substitute instead. The Stone's reappearance in Arbroath Abbey in April 1951 was followed by further uncertainty. Was this the same Stone that had been taken from Westminster Abbey four months before, or a replica? Were the authorities fooled into accepting the return of a fake Stone, leaving the genuine Stone in Scotland, its whereabouts known only to a handful of Scottish nationalists? This scenario forms the basis of persistent doubts about the Stone's authenticity and is central to its modern mythology.

There is, indeed, not only a second 'Stone', but probably several others. All, however, are twentieth-century copies of the genuine Stone and few, if any, are likely to be confused with the genuine article. These include one made in 1984 and displayed on the Moot Hill at Scone for the benefit of visitors (**colour plate 12**). But it is the first copy of the Stone, made in 1929, that has sparked most controversy. This was made by Robert ('Bertie') Gray (**62**), a monumental sculptor and Glasgow city councillor, in preparation for an aborted attempt to take the Stone from Westminster Abbey. In 1950, Gray was entrusted with repairing the real Stone after it was damaged during its removal from the Coronation Chair. According to popular tradition, Gray also used the opportunity presented by his unrestricted access to the Stone to make another, better copy. But the two stones became mixed up and even the perpetrators were unable to distinguish between them. As a result, they were unaware which stone was left at Arbroath Abbey and subsequently returned to Westminster.

31 *The Knights Templar remove their 'Stone of Destiny' from St Columba's Church, Dundee*

Alternatively, a copy of the Stone was deliberately left at Arbroath Abbey for the authorities to recover and return to Westminster, leaving the real Stone in the hands of those who took it. A stone is then said to have 'turned up' in Parliament Square, Edinburgh in 1965 and, at a meeting of Scottish nationalists held to decide its fate, Gray claimed that this was the real Stone. The Rev John Mackay Nimmo, of St Columba's Church, Dundee, agreed to keep the stone in his church. Nimmo was also Chaplain to the Scottish Knights Templar of the Chivalric Military Order of the Temple of Jerusalem, founded in the nineteenth century as the Militia Templi Scotia to maintain the Scottish Templar and Jacobite freemasonry traditions. The Knights' secret history allegedly refers to four sacred stones and the Knights believe that the stone entrusted to Nimmo is one of these, the genuine Stone of Destiny. On the closure of St Columba's Church in 1990, the stone was transferred to the Knights' new church, at Dull, Perthshire (**31, 33**). But when it was examined by the People's Palace, Glasgow, in 1990, no traces of the repairs that Gray made in 1951 were detected. Moreover, there was no trace of the natural flaw which had broken in 1950, only an artificial 'crack', chiselled into the Stone's surface. The 'Knights' Stone' is not the stone that was removed from Westminster Abbey in 1950 and may be dismissed as a fake.

On its return to Westminster Abbey in 1951, the Stone was examined in detail and compared with earlier photographs. This revealed it to be the same Stone that had been removed from the Coronation Chair some four months previously. This is corroborated by Ian Hamilton, who led the group that took the Stone and has consistently stated that the Stone taken from Westminster Abbey was the same as that returned. Moreover, the Dean and Chapter of Westminster Abbey were never in any doubt that the real Stone was returned, not only in 1951, but also when the 'Knights' Stone' appeared in 1965. The case for the authenticity of the Stone is overwhelming. The Stone moved to Edinburgh Castle in 1996 is neither a fake nor a 'double fake'. Instead, the evidence supports the conclusion

32 *The Knights Templar's 'Stone of Destiny' on the move*

that Edward I took the genuine Stone from Scone in 1296 and that, following its removal in 1950, this same Stone was returned to Westminster Abbey. Nevertheless, the issue resurfaced in 2008, when Scotland's First Minister, Alex Salmond, voiced his doubts about the authenticity of the Stone.

Despite this evidence, the controversy surrounding its authenticity is now an integral part of the Stone's modern mythology. Claim and counter-claim will presumably continue unabated. In the perceived absence of conclusive information and hard facts about the Stone's authenticity, a growing number of increasingly implausible interpretations have emerged to fill the void. The Stone's very nature – ancient, mysterious, symbolic, emotive, internationally famous, and the subject of a plethora of myths and traditions – means that it will always attract such theories. This is part of the richness of the Stone's history and, if any was required, an undeniable indication of the Stone's continued relevance, particularly to the Scots. In a very tangible sense the Stone belongs to everyone. Anyone can advance their own theories about the origins, function, symbolism and authenticity of the Stone and, over the years, many have.

5

THE STONE AT SCONE

But what excites the curiosity of every person who has been interested in reading the history of Scotland, and attracts the attention of almost every traveller, is Scone.

[*Old*] *Statistical Account*, vol. 18 (1796)

Scone, venerable to every Scotsman as the seat of royalty ... this almost sacred ground.

James Robertson, *General View of the Agriculture in the County of Perth* (1799)

The Stone of Destiny originated near Scone and its earliest reliably recorded location is at Scone. Scone is therefore central to our understanding of the Stone, its function and symbolic significance. What was Scone, why was it important and why was the Stone kept there? And, if the Stone's presence was so significant, what happened to Scone after it was removed?

Scone (pronounced *skoon*) (National Grid Reference NO 1355 2655) is located on the east bank of the River Tay, 1.2 miles (2km) north of Perth. It occupies a slight eminence on an elevated alluvial terrace overlooking a bend in the Tay and its confluence with the River Almond (**33, 34**). The site is now dominated by Scone Palace, the seat of the earls of Mansfield (**colour plate 13**).

EARLY MEDIEVAL SCONE

Scone was a Scottish and, before that, probably a Pictish royal power centre, 'the place where both the Pictish and the Scottish kings from ancient times had established the chief seat of their kingdom', according to Fordun. Although this is partially supported by early medieval sources, Scone's early history is obscure and there are problems of identification. The Irish annals record a battle between Pictish factions in 728 at *Castellum Credi* or *Caislen Credi* ('the fortress of Crede'), which some historians identify with the *Collis Credulitatis*, the Moot Hill at Scone. However, *Crede* is not related to *Credulitatis*, but is a personal name, and there is no evidence of a fortified site at Scone. *Castellum Credi* remains unidentified, although the fact that the battle was for the Pictish kingship may indicate that it was fought near a royal centre, for which Irish parallels exist.

Another place sometimes identified with Scone is *Cinnbelathoir*. Donald I (858–62) died in the palace at *Cinnbelathoir*, according to the source formerly known as the *Scottish Chronicle* but now usually referred to as the *Chronicle of the Kings of Alba*. But Fordun and

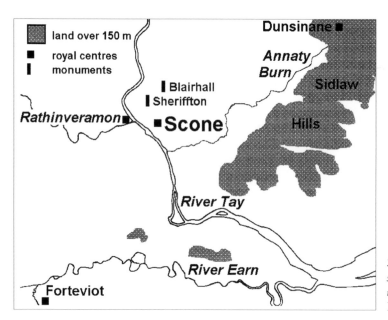

33 *The Scone area, showing locations mentioned in the text.* Nick Aitchison

the *Prose and Verse Chronicle* inserted in the *Chronicle of Melrose* place Donald's death at Scone, which was then 'the seat of royalty' (*sedem regiam*), according to Fordun. These, however, are later sources and may reflect Scone's medieval significance. There is no evidence to equate *Cinnbelathoir* with Scone; it may be another name for the royal centre of *Rathinveramon* (Inveralmond) which is named as Donald's place of death in some versions of the Pictish regnal lists. *Rathinveramon* is possibly located on the site of the Roman fort at Bertha, 0.9 miles (1.5km) west of Scone (**33, 34**).

Scone lies within a landscape of prehistoric monuments dating from as early as the Neolithic period (*c*.3500–2200 BC). These monuments include a barrow cemetery and cursus (a linear earthwork perhaps forming a ceremonial avenue) at Blairhall, 0.75 miles (1.2km) north of Scone (**34**), and a cemetery of two circular and four square barrows at Sherifftown, 1 mile (1.5km) north-west of Scone. Possibly Pictish square barrows also occur within an extensive complex of prehistoric ritual monuments at the royal centre of Forteviot (**35**). This juxtaposition not only indicates that prehistoric monuments were perceived to be important during the early medieval period, but attests an active appropriation of the past. Scone's origins as a royal centre may lie in the exploitation of nearby prehistoric monuments for political advantage by a Pictish socio-political élite and their incorporation within early medieval rituals of royalty.

Although they are uncorroborated, later sources consistently portray Scone as a Pictish royal centre. Scone is the setting of the violent takeover of the Pictish kingdom by the Scots under Kenneth mac Alpín (843–58), an event traditionally dated to 843. Several medieval accounts relate how the Pictish nobles invited their Scottish counterparts to a feast at Scone. Once their hosts were drunk, the Scots removed the pins supporting the benches the Picts were sitting on. Trapped in the recesses underneath, the Picts were then killed by their guests.

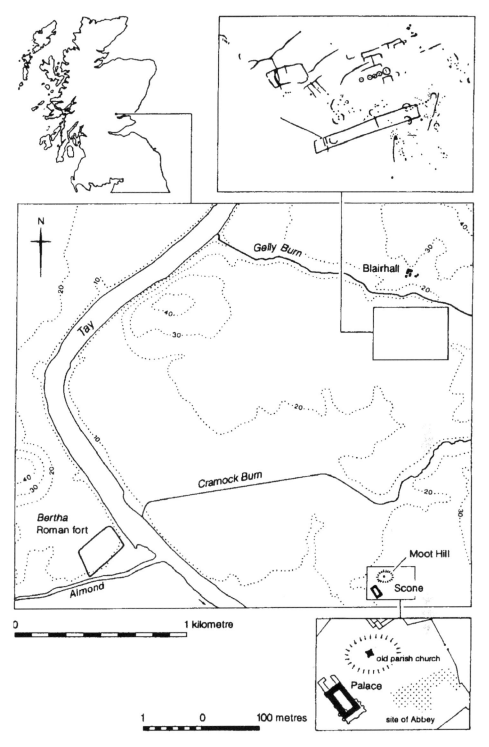

34 *Scone, showing its proximity to the prehistoric and Pictish monumental complex at Blairhall.*
Dr Stephen Driscoll

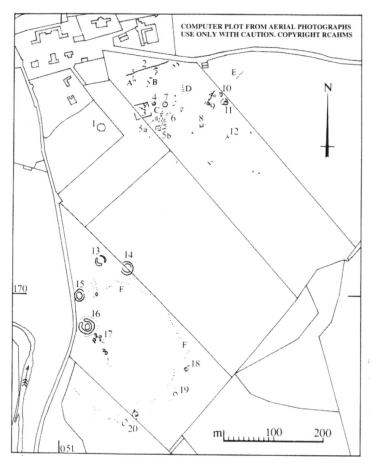

35 *Forteviot, Perthshire, a transcribed plan of the cropmark complex. Cropmarks reveal the presence of probably Pictish square barrows amidst the prehistoric ritual complex of much larger henge monuments.* Copyright: Royal Commission on the Ancient and Historical Monuments of Scotland

This tale belongs to an older tradition and features in the eleventh-century *Prophecy of Berchán*, a verse history of Scottish and Irish kings. This foretold of Kenneth that:

> The men in the east [the Picts] are deceived by him,
> They dig the earth, mighty the occupation,
> A deadly goad-pit, death by wounding,
> In the middle of Scone of the high shields.

The *Book of Leinster* refers to a lost tenth-century Irish tale, *The Treachery of Scone* (*Braflang Scóine*), which presumably concerns the same event. Influenced by this tradition, later versions of the Pictish regnal lists record that the last Pictish king, Drust son of Ferat, was 'killed at Scone by treason', attributing his murder to the Scots, although earlier versions place his death at Forteviot.

This tradition has a distinctly mythological appearance. It attempts to explain the Picts' disappearance and the Scots' dominance with a single event, the Scots' elimination of the Pictish nobility at Scone. The reality was more complex. The Picts were assimilated rather than conquered by the Scots by *c*.900. This was the culmination of processes that had begun by the early eighth century, including the intermarriage of the Pictish and Scottish royal lines, the eastward movement of Scottish settlers and the spread of the Gaelic language. Coupled with the weakening of the Picts from wars against both the Scots and the Vikings, these processes led ultimately to the Picts' absorption by the Scots. The 'treachery of Scone' represents an invented, mythological past.

Kenneth was 'the first king of the Scots to take the kingdom of Scone (*righe Sgoinde*)', according to the *Synchronisms of Fland Mainistrech*, an eleventh-century Irish king list. Scone is referred to metaphorically, the royal centre symbolising the kingdom to which it belonged. But which kingdom? Scone is in the province of Gowrie which, with Strathearn and Menteith, was encompassed by the Pictish kingdom of Fortriu (**36**). Although a recent claim that Fortriu was located in Northern Pictland, around the Moray Firth, has gained wide acceptance, it is not followed here. The earliest reference to a king of *Fortriu* is in 693, when the *Annals of Tigernach* record the death of a *rex Fortrenn*. By the ninth century, the kingship of Fortriu was synonymous with that of the Picts as a whole. Scone may have originated as a royal centre of the kings of Fortriu and, as those kings extended their power, acquired a wider significance within Pictland.

Despite this, there is no recorded archaeological evidence to confirm Scone's status as a Pictish royal centre. Placenames also provide few clues. There is a concentration of placenames of Pictish origin in south-east Perthshire, including that of Perth (*pert* 'wood', 'copse') itself. The most common and, in terms of identifying Pictish settlement, significant placenames include the element Pit-, formed from *pett*, meaning '(dependent) estate'. Only one *pit*-placename, *Pitculen*, is recorded in the Scone area. As with almost all surviving *pit*-placenames, this is combined with a Gaelic element, revealing that it was coined after Gaelic had become the dominant language in eastern central Scotland, *c*. 900. Several *bal*-placenames, derived from *baile*, the Gaelic equivalent of Pictish *pit*, are also recorded near Scone, attesting the existence of dependent estates around the royal centre in the period before *c*. 1100.

Paradoxically, the best indicator of Scone's status as a Pictish royal centre is its association with the early Scottish kingship, which probably occupied pre-existing Pictish royal centres. This may have been partly for pragmatic reasons, enabling the newly-ascendant

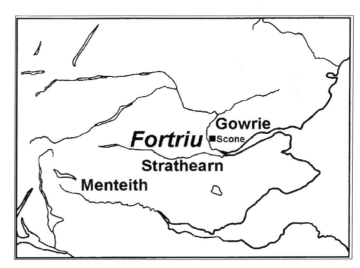

36 *Central Scotland, showing the location of the Pictish kingdom of* Fortriu, *comprising the provinces of Gowrie, Menteith and Strathearn.*
Nick Aitchison

Scottish kingship to reuse existing sites and their buildings and exploit established socio-economic relations, ensuring the supply of everything from food renders to skilled craftsmen. But earlier royal centres were also reoccupied for symbolic or ideological reasons: these locations and their monuments embodied royal pasts. By acquiring Pictish power centres and adopting their associated royal rituals, the early Scottish kings were legitimising their newly-extended power over Pictland by appropriating the aura and mystique of royal power conferred by these royal places. This *may* have included the appropriation of Pictish inauguration rituals involving the Stone.

Scone's status as an early Scottish royal centre is apparent from the *Chronicle of the Kings of Alba*:

> in his sixth year [906], King Constantine [II] and Bishop Cellach, on the Hill of Faith (*collis credulitatis*) near the royal city (*regali cívitati*) of Scone, pledged themselves that the laws and disciplines of the faith, and the rights in churches and gospels, should be kept in conformity with [the customs of] the Scots. From that day the hill has deserved this name ... the Hill of Faith.

This may have imposed Scottish liturgical practices and ecclesiastical law on Pictish churches and was therefore an event of national importance.

Scone's description as a *regali cívitati* is significant. Bede refers to Dumbarton Rock and Bamburgh, the fortified royal centres of the Strathclyde Britons and Northumbrians respectively, as *civitates*. The *Life of Bishop Wilfrid* by Eddius Stephanus records the progress of King Ecgfrith of Northumbria (670–85) through 'chief towns, forts and townships' (*civitates et castella vicosque*), implying a hierarchy with *civitates* at the top. In Northumbria at least, *civitas* denoted the principal place in a kingdom, while the *Chronicle of the Kings of Alba* indicates that Scone was the pre-eminent royal power centre in *Alba*.

Scone's importance is also apparent from its prominence in the *Prophecy of Berchán*. In addition to Kenneth's slaughter of the Picts at Scone, the *Prophecy* states of Constantine III (995–97) that 'weak men will be around him in the territory of Scone of the high shields' and prophesies (inaccurately) that Macbeth (1040–57) will die 'in the middle of Scone'. That Scone was considered an appropriate setting for Macbeth's death emphasises its status as the principal royal centre and inauguration place of the Scottish kings during Macbeth's reign.

But Scone was not the 'capital' of Pictland or *Alba*. This common misconception originates with Fordun's description of Scone as 'the chief seat of the kingdom' of the Picts and Scots. The concept of capital cities is a modern one. Throughout the Middle Ages, kingship was peripatetic in nature; kings and their retinues travelled around the kingdom, living off food renders from their subjects, collecting tribute, making laws and dispensing justice. Embodied in the person of the king, the kingdom's administrative and legal centre moved between royal centres, one of which was Scone. Some probably performed specialised functions, utilitarian or symbolic, or were favoured by certain kings for specific activities, such as hunting, or for spending certain times of the year, particularly the major Christian festivals.

Each royal centre and its estates were administered by a royal official. It is from this pre-feudal system of Pictish socio-economic and territorial organisation that the administrative unit known as the 'thanage' emerged in north-eastern Scotland during the twelfth century. Scone was described as a royal manor during Malcolm IV's reign and would have been managed by a (probably hereditary) thane or *toísech*, the basic noble rank in Scotland during this period, although the earliest record of Scone as a thanage is not until 1234. Scone's role as a legislative centre is apparent from the proclamation of 906 and the royal charters granted there throughout the medieval period. Early medieval administrative centres frequently became the location of later gallows and this is attested by a placename, Gallows Knowe, at Scone.

There is no recorded archaeological evidence to supplement the meagre documentary sources for early medieval Scone. Although the construction of the medieval abbey and later palace probably damaged any early medieval remains, archaeology presents considerable potential for enhancing our understanding of the Pictish and early Scottish royal centre. Scone's description as a 'royal town' implies an extensive complex, probably comprising royal halls, domestic and ancillary buildings and a church, possibly within an enclosure.

Scone has been claimed as the site of the stone church built for Nechtan by Ceolfrith's builders in 710, although there is no evidence to corroborate this. The close links between kingship and Church, exemplified by the proclamation of 906, indicate that there was a royal church at Scone, at least by that date. As at Forteviot, where a magnificent sculptured arch from a probably ninth-century royal church was found (15), this may have been of stone. Like other Scottish royal and ecclesiastical centres, notably Dunkeld and St Andrews, a community of *Céli Dé* ('Servants of God', scotticised as Culdees), an ascetic revival movement originating in eighth-century Ireland, was established at Scone sometime between the ninth and eleventh centuries. Further evidence of an early ecclesiastical site at or near Scone is provided by the Annaty Burn, 0.8 mile (1.3km) south-east of Scone. This derives its name from the placename element *annaid*, denoting the church of a patron saint or church containing the relics of its founder.

Although the evidence is fragmentary, Scone was evidently a royal centre of exceptional importance from at least the early tenth century and a range of ceremonial, domestic, religious, fiscal and judicial functions were probably performed there. Scone was probably also an elaborate palace complex, providing royal accommodation, an assembly place, an administrative centre for controlling the landscape's resources and collecting food renders and taxes from royal estates, and a court for the administration of justice. These functions emerge more clearly from the twelfth century. Scone was an elaborate theatre for the display of royal power and inauguration rituals were probably integral to the activities performed there from an early date.

SCONE ABBEY

Scone emerges as an important ecclesiastical centre during the twelfth century with the foundation of a priory and its elevation to an abbey. In 1114, Alexander I founded a stone- built monastic church at Scone in gratitude to God for delivering him from 'certain ruffians of the Mearns and Moray', as Fordun relates. The *Chronicle of Melrose* records that 'The church of Scone was given over to canons', indicating the transformation of a pre-existing *Céli Dé* community, as at other ecclesiastical centres in eastern central Scotland. The six canons regular and their prior came from the Church of St Oswald at Nastlay, near Pontefract in Yorkshire, to establish an Augustinian community at Scone.

Alexander's church was dedicated to the Holy Trinity and St Michael the Archangel by Bishop Turgot of St Andrews. Fordun describes how 'almost the whole of the kingdom flocked' to the ceremony, but adds that these crowds attended 'by the king's command'. Implying that Scone was then one of the three most important royal churches in Scotland, Alexander endowed the churches at Scone, Dunfermline and St Andrews 'with many great gifts' and that at Scone with 'many great privileges', according to Fordun. These privileges included the abbey's entitlement to skins, hides, fat and bread from the king's household and to levy 'cain' (tribute) from ships berthing at Scone. Alexander also informed English merchants of the abbey's right to bring ships to Scone free of customs duties. Alexander and later kings also granted to Scone Abbey the right to teinds (tithes) of agricultural products from several royal estates in Perthshire and Angus.

In 1124, Alexander granted jurisdiction to the prior and brethren of Scone. The Augustinian communities of Scone and St Andrews were closely linked and Robert, Scone's first prior, became bishop of St Andrews the same year. After recovering from a serious illness, Malcolm IV enriched Scone Priory with further privileges in 1163. The priory was elevated to an abbacy around the same time and, in 1164, Pope Alexander III confirmed the abbey's possessions in a charter to Robert, Abbot of the 'Church of the Blessed Michael of Scone'. Scone's continuing importance as an ecclesiastical and royal centre is confirmed by an assembly of prelates, earls, barons and freeholders of Scotland at Scone in 1209. There, William proclaimed the Church's freedom from secular interference: 'the holy Scottish Church, the holy religion, and entire clergy should be maintained, with all their rights, liberties, and privileges, in quiet peace, and always under royal protection'.

A document in the Scone chartulary gives an impression of the abbey buildings soon after the Stone was taken. In 1298, Abbot Thomas of Scone complained that the English army had smashed the ceilings, roofs, doors and windows of the church, refectory, dormitory, cloisters and chambers. They had also broken open cupboards, chests, caskets and locks and had ripped the seals from, then either destroyed or stolen, a large number of royal charters confirming the abbey's rights and possessions dating back to the reign of David I. And in 1365 the abbey comprised a church, cloisters, refectory, *capitulum*, and hospital, all within a monastic boundary inside which no women were admitted. The hospital, a hostel for visiting pilgrims, is first recorded in a charter of 1206–1227. There was also an adjacent secular settlement, the *villa de Scona*, with its inns and bothies, which would have provided labour and services for the abbey.

The abbey has not survived as an upstanding monument. Its remains were either reused as building materials for the baronial 'palace' or removed when the palace grounds were landscaped. In 1796, 'the vestiges of the old abbey church about 100 yards due east from the south-east corner of the house' were still visible, according to the [*Old*] *Statistical Account*. This suggests that it stood near the western end of the present burial ground, although the topography of the site led the Royal Commission on the Ancient and Historical Monuments of Scotland to believe that the burial ground occupies the site of the abbey church (**37**). The *New Statistical Account* records that, in 1841, alterations to

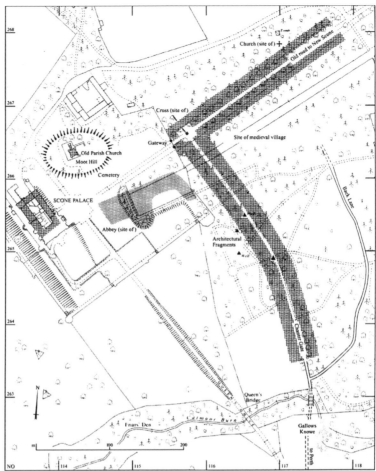

37 *Plan of Scone Palace and its environs.* Copyright: Royal Commission on the Ancient and Historical Monuments of Scotland

a garden terrace on the south side of the burial ground exposed 'one apartment, which seemed to be a sort of cell ... surrounded by stone seats'. As the cloisters typically occupied this area in medieval abbeys, this may have belonged to a claustral range. Little else is known about the abbey buildings. The only visible traces are some scattered architectural fragments (**38**). Although the archaeological investigation of Scone Abbey has only just begun, initial results are encouraging. Geophysical survey and trial excavation located the remains of the abbey church and cloister in 2007 and 2008.

Scone's archaeological potential is indicated by the remains of its cemetery. In 1841, 'two stone coffins in good preservation' were discovered near the 'sort of cell', according to the *New Statistical Account*. Furthermore, 'a great many stone coffins, some rough, and others in some degree hewn, in which the skeletons were very entire', as well as 'many skeletons without any coffin', were exposed 'between the present palace and the churchyard' in 1841–43. The different burial rites recorded suggests either a difference in the social status of those buried there or that these burials belong to different periods. The abbey church itself would have been reserved for the burial of royalty and senior clerics;

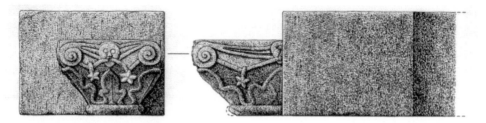

38 *A Romanesque cubic capital, probably from a door or window of the priory church at Scone, built in 1114. This is one of several surviving architectural fragments from the medieval ecclesiastical buildings there.* Copyright: Royal Commission on the Ancient and Historical Monuments of Scotland

Matilda (Maud), queen of David I, died at Scone in 1131 and was buried in a tomb in the church, evidence of its status as a royal church. This church played an important role in other rituals of royalty, including inauguration ceremonies.

EARLY INAUGURATION

Inauguration ceremonies were fundamental to the concept and practice of medieval kingship, demonstrating the legitimacy of a monarch's rule by invoking notions of divine kingship and appealing to the past. Inauguration according to traditional and accepted practice was an explicit acknowledgement of a king's hereditary right to the throne and established his status as a just and lawful ruler. By this means, kings sought to project their kingship as unchallengeable. Royal inauguration ceremonies were not only a means of ritually transmitting rank, but were also a strategy of legitimisation in ensuring that the king retained his position.

Inauguration rituals assumed a greater significance in early medieval Scotland and Ireland because of their system of royal succession. Instead of primogeniture, in which sons directly succeeded their fathers, the kingship alternated between collateral lines of the royal kin group (**39**). As that kin group grew in size over time it also became increasingly unstable as rival candidates struggled for the kingship. This instability was exacerbated by attempts to discard alternating succession in favour of primogeniture, resulting in Duncan I succeeding his grandfather Malcolm II in 1034 and precipitating Duncan's murder by Macbeth in 1040. Within a system of royal succession that was inherently unstable and frequently resulted in dynastic strife, inauguration rituals provided an important means of demonstrating the king's right to the throne and of deterring potential challengers, at least in theory.

After the adoption of primogeniture, the tendency of Scottish kings to inherit the throne in their infancy was a cause of further instability. Royal nervousness is reflected in attempts to have heirs recognised. In 1152, David I commanded that his eldest grandson, the future Malcolm IV, 'should be conducted round the provinces of Scotland and proclaimed to be the heir to the kingdom', according to John of Hexham. Malcolm was accompanied by Duncan – who, as Earl of Fife, was hereditarily responsible for inaugurating the future

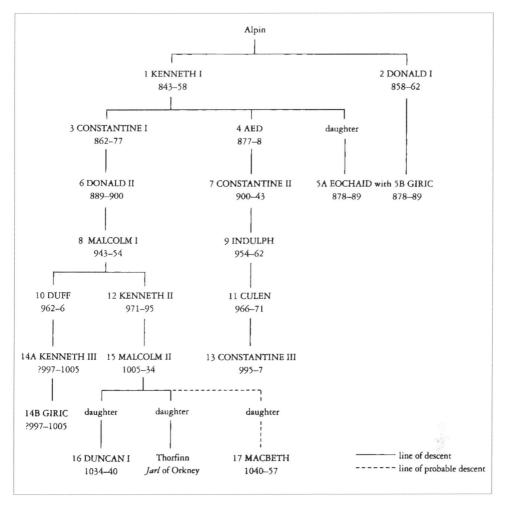

39 *Genealogical table of Scotland's early kings, 843–1057. The numbered sequence reveals the system of alternating succession between collateral branches of the royal kin group.* Nick Aitchison

king – and 'a numerous army'. More commonly, the heir probably gained acceptance at an assembly where an oath of fealty or loyalty was sworn, such as that held by William in 1201 to acknowledge his three year old son, the future Alexander II, as heir. But the issue still troubled William on his deathbed in 1214, when he sought assurances that Alexander would be accepted as his successor.

Early Scottish kings were installed at Scone. Although obscure, Scone's origins as an inauguration site are important to understanding the royal centre and as a possible indication of the Stone's earliest presence there. Scone may have originated as a Pictish inauguration site, firstly of the kings of Fortriu and later of all Pictland. The early Scottish kings probably appropriated this Pictish inauguration place, drawing on the legitimacy conferred by their association with an ancient royal site as a means of consolidating their rule over their newly-enlarged kingdom.

40 *A woodcut illustration from Holinshed's* Chronicles *(1577) showing the Elizabethan perception of early inauguration ceremonies in terms of contemporary coronation rites. The king whose 'coronation' is depicted here is Macbeth (1040–57)*

The earliest recorded inaugurations at Scone are of Giric (878–89) and Donald II (889–900). 'When this Giric had obtained rule over the kingdom with the consent of most of the magnates, he was solemnly crowned at Scone', receiving the kingship in an unspecified 'ceremony of coronation', according to Fordun. Fordun also records that 'the supreme position in the kingdom was obtained by Donald ... and he was crowned at Scone'. But Fordun's late, uncorroborated and anachronistic account simply projects the medieval coronation rite some five centuries into the past, as other chroniclers did (**40**). Nevertheless, Fordun was expressing a medieval perception of Scone as an inauguration place of great antiquity.

An archaic and distinctive feature of early Scottish kingship is that kings were not crowned but installed in an apparently ancient ritual which, according to later accounts, involved being enthroned on the Stone or a throne holding it. But little is known about these early ceremonies. Although Scone's status as an inauguration centre appears to be of great antiquity, there are no reliable records of any inaugurations before the twelfth century and the earliest to be recorded in any detail was not until 1249. It is unsurprising, therefore, that there are no early references to the Stone or the role it played in royal inaugurations.

Twelfth-century references to inaugurations at Scone contain few details, making Ailred's comments about David I's inauguration in 1124 all the more intriguing. Ailred, a member of David's household and later abbot of Rievaulx, Yorkshire, recorded that:

> we know that he [David I] sought not the kingship, but abhorred it, and did rather receive it because of outward necessity than seize upon it greedily, conquered by

the lust of reigning. And hence he so abhorred those acts of homage (*obsequia*) which are offered by the Scottish nation in the manner of their fathers upon the recent promotion of their kings, that he was with difficulty compelled by the bishops to receive them.

Speculation about the nature of those unspecified rituals has been fuelled by a description of an Irish inauguration ritual in Giraldus Cambrensis' *Topography of Ireland* (*Topographia Hiberniae*) (1188–89). This describes how the king of 'a certain people' among the *Cenél Conaill* in what is now County Donegal had sexual intercourse with a mare which was then sacrificed and made into broth. The king then bathed in the broth, which he and his assembled people consumed (**colour plate 14**).

Regardless of the reliability of Giraldus' account, David's inauguration is most unlikely to have involved anything as outlandish. Unspecified bishops persuaded David to be inaugurated in the traditional manner, according to Ailred, indicating that there was already an established and prominent ecclesiastical element to the ceremony by 1124. Such practices may already have been ancient, as Columba's 'ordination' of Aedán as king of Dál Riata in 574 suggests. David's reaction was probably prompted by his long absence at the English court, from 1100, when his sister Matilda married Henry I, to his accession in 1124. From David's anglicised perspective, the Scottish royal inauguration ceremony may have seemed either uncivilised or simply unfashionable. But Ailred also used the incident to illustrate David's humility. There is no evidence that Scottish kings were inaugurated in a primitive 'tribal' ritual. Indeed, the bishops' pressure on David to conform to a traditional inauguration ritual attests a formal and conspicuous ecclesiastical dimension. The presence of an early church at Scone and the close relationship between kingship and Church indicates that there was an explicitly Christian component to the inauguration ritual from an early date.

Scottish inaugurations gradually become better documented from the mid-twelfth century and a composite picture may be constructed tentatively from references to specific elements of the ceremonies performed at Scone. In 1153, 'all the people of the land, raising up Malcolm [IV] ... established him as king at Scone, as is the custom of that nation', according to John of Hexham. That the inauguration was conducted not only in the presence of, but *by*, 'all the people of the land' suggests that the king was inaugurated in an assembly by popular acclaim. Malcolm's 'raising up' may have been physical and/or metaphorical, onto the Stone, a throne, or the Moot Hill, the mound on which inaugurations were conducted, or a combination of these. This is reminiscent of the *Prophecy of Berchán*'s references to 'Scone of the high shields' (*Scoinne sciath airde*), which may allude to the raising of newly-installed kings shoulder-high above the assembled throng, while 'Scone of melodious shields' (*Scoinne sciath bhinne*) may refer to the acclamation of the new king by beating shields. But it is unclear what Hexham was referring to as customary: the ritual, its location, or both.

Ecclesiastical participation in William's inauguration in 1165 is also recorded. Fordun describes how 'the prelates and magnates of the kingdom came together at Scone and unanimously chose as their king the noble William'. That the ceremony was conducted by a secular and ecclesiastical élite contrasts with Malcolm's inauguration by 'all the people of the land', indicating a shift from inauguration by public acclamation to a more exclusive ceremony. This marks the increasing 'mystification' of kingship as the social distance between kings and their subjects was extended.

Alexander II's inauguration, on 6 December 1214, provides an insight into the timing of the inauguration and the events surrounding it, rather than the nature of the ritual itself. Fordun relates how William was taken ill and died 'After he had commended his son Alexander to the bishops, earls and barons as their future king and they had accepted him as such'. Then:

> the next day after the king's death, very early in the morning, while Walter, Bishop of Glasgow, Robert, [Bishop] Elect of Ross, the queen, William of Boscho, the Chancellor, and a good many of his household, abode with the deceased king's body, the earls of Fife, Strathearn, Atholl, Angus, Menteith, Buchan and Lothian, together with William, Bishop of St Andrews, took the king's son, Alexander, a lad of 16 years, and, bringing him as far as Scone, they raised him to the throne, in honour and peace, with the approval of God and man, and with more grandeur and glory than any one until then, while all wished him joy, and none denied him. So King Alexander, as was fitting, held his feast in state, at Scone, on that day (that is to say, Friday), and the Saturday following (namely, the feast of St Nicholas), as well as the next Sunday. On the Monday, at the bridge of Perth, he met his father's body, which was being taken down, in great state, to Arbroath, to be buried, as the king himself, before his death, had directed.

The *Chronicle of Melrose* records that, two days after William's death, Alexander 'proceeded to Scone with no small assemblage of magnates; and there, both peacefully and honourably, in royal fashion and with fitting ceremony, he received the government of the kingdom of Scotland'.

Continuity of kingship was essential. Alexander was not only named as William's successor before the king's death, but his acceptance by the magnates and senior clerics indicates that this was done before the assembled secular and ecclesiastical hierarchies. As kingship was measured from a king's inauguration, not the death of his predecessor, it was essential for the heir apparent to act quickly on his predecessor's death. Indeed, the nobles' haste to get Alexander to Scone and installed in the kingship before William's body was buried might seem indecent. But avoiding an interregnum was paramount. As the king personified the state and its powers, an interregnum constituted a grave crisis; there could be no king's peace without a king. As Fordun records Walter Comyn's warning before the inauguration of Alexander III in 1249, 'just as a boat is tossed about among the waves without an oarsman, so a kingdom without a king or ruler is left in the lurch'. The transition to the new kingship was completed, and the powers of the newly-installed king emphasised, by the king presiding over a parliament at Scone on the day after his inauguration.

Alexander II's inauguration is the first to be recorded as an enthronement. Although there is no reference to the Stone, this may parallel Alexander III's enthronement on the

Stone in 1249. The practice of enthronement may mirror earlier rituals; it was presumably a throne onto which Malcolm IV was raised. But the scale of Alexander II's inauguration ceremony appears to have differed from previous rituals; Fordun describes an occasion of great pomp and circumstance, culminating in three days of feasting. Again, this may attest the growing 'mystification' of the kingship, resulting in increasingly elaborate and exclusive inauguration, and other royal, rituals.

The ecclesiastical and secular elements of the inauguration ceremony now begin to emerge. Alexander was made king 'with the approval of God and man' and Scotland's senior cleric, the bishop of St Andrews, played a central though unspecified role. The earls of Fife and Strathearn head Fordun's list of magnates, indicating their seniority and central role in the ceremony. The MacDuff Earls of Fife belonged to a collateral branch of the royal kin group, descended from the eponymous Dub (or Duff), king of Scots (962–66). Although excluded from eligibility to the kingship in the early eleventh century, the loyalty of the earls of Fife was retained and rewarded with a prominent political role, as Scotland's senior noble and kingmaker. The earls of Strathearn may have occupied a similar position or owe their prominence to their earldom's proximity to Scone.

In their continuous quest for prestige and legitimacy, Scottish kings sought new rituals and regalia. Influenced by Anglo-Norman and, ultimately, continental practices, these rituals included coronation and anointment, the smearing of the new monarch with holy oil blessed by the pope. Alexander II unsuccessfully asked to be crowned and anointed by a visiting papal legate in 1221 and was again refused the right to anointment in 1233. From the reign of Edgar (1097–1107), most Scottish royal seals depict kings wearing crowns (**17-23, 25**), as do twelfth-century coins. And both David and his grandson and successor, Malcolm IV, are depicted with crowns in a charter granted by Malcolm to Kelso Abbey in 1159 (**colour plate 15**). But although Scottish kings wore crowns, they were not crowned in an ecclesiastical ceremony with anointing or unction. Medieval kings craved prestige, and coronation and anointment were potent and international symbols of royal status and authority. However, successive English kings, anxious to deny their Scottish counterparts equal status, successfully pressurised the pope into denying Scottish kings the right to anointment.

THE INAUGURATION OF ALEXANDER III

Our knowledge of the medieval Scottish inauguration ritual and, by implication, its earlier forms comes from Fordun's and Bower's accounts of Alexander III's installation. Both are based on independent first hand accounts, although Bower anachronistically describes the ceremony as a coronation. Bower's source, which he preferred to Fordun's, was probably a record kept in St Andrews and provides some additional information not present in Fordun's account but omits other details. The two descriptions differ in their ordering of events, with Bower giving the more likely sequence; according to Fordun, the king was enthroned immediately and only consecrated afterwards.

Remarkably, two illustrations of Alexander's inauguration also survive. One is on a seal of Scone Abbey, which was probably struck soon after the inauguration, and the other is in a mid-fifteenth-century manuscript of Bower's *Scotichronicon* (**41**; **colour plate 16**).

Used in conjunction, these literary and pictorial sources provide a unique insight into the Scottish royal inauguration ritual. And, for the first time, the Stone's presence and function in the inauguration ceremony are revealed.

Alexander II died on the island of Kerrera, Argyll, while campaigning to extend royal authority over the western isles and was buried at Melrose on 8 July 1249. Alexander's son, also called Alexander, was only eight years old. On 13 July 1249, the young Alexander travelled to Scone with several earls, barons and knights, where they were met by David de Bernham, Bishop of St Andrews, Geoffrey, Bishop of Dunkeld, and the abbot of Scone. Scone was then 'the chief seat of the kingdom' (*superiori sede regni Scona*), according to Fordun, although little is known of the form it took.

Two controversies rapidly arose amongst the assembled magnates. Some claimed that it was an inauspicious day, on which Alexander could be knighted but not made king. The instigator was Sir Alan Durward, Justiciar of Scotland, who was probably motivated by an ambition to become regent. The debate also reflects the growing influence of English concepts of kingship and knighthood. Scottish chroniclers claimed inaccurately that, in 1087, William II of England had been knighted before being crowned the same day, although these events were actually a decade apart. But Henry III of England, who – like Alexander – became king while still a boy, was knighted before his coronation in 1216. Walter Comyn, Earl of Menteith, resolved the argument, proposing that the ceremony proceed forthwith and that Alexander should be knighted before being installed in the kingship. The magnates gave their approval, perhaps indicating that Alexander was publicly acclaimed before being inaugurated.

The ceremony began when the bishop of St Andrews 'girded the king with the belt of knighthood'. Bower describes how the royal inauguration oath then followed. The bishop of St Andrews 'set out the rights and promises which pertain to a king, first in Latin and then in French, the king graciously conceded and accepted all of this, and

41 *The inauguration of Alexander III, 1249, as depicted on the seal of Scone Abbey.* W. de G. Birch, *History of Scottish Seals*

42 *The Moot Hill at Scone, from the south. The church stands in the centre of this low, flat-topped earthen mound.* Nick Aitchison

readily underwent and permitted his blessing and ordination at the hands of the same bishop'. 'Blessing and ordination' are probably the liturgical terms for the inauguration's ecclesiastical component, which suggests that they were performed inside the abbey church. Fordun describes this part of the ceremony as 'consecration' and places it after the enthronement.

The next stage in the ceremony was held outdoors, as the seal's stippled background indicates. The bishops and some nobles led Alexander to a point 'in front of the cross that stands in the graveyard at the east end of the church'. But the cross concerned has not survived and there is some confusion about the precise location. The illustration shows the inauguration ceremony in progress in front of a cross on top, or in front, of a large flat-topped mound. This is almost certainly the Moot Hill (**42, 43**), although it lies north, not east, of the abbey's probable site, where Fordun and Bower both place the ceremony. No other mounds are recorded at Scone and the range of royal activities associated with the Moot Hill indicates that this was the feature concerned. Although the illustration appears to place the ceremony beside the mound, this may reflect artistic licence, the illustrator having insufficient space towards the top of the page. Alexander III was probably inaugurated on the Moot Hill; if not, his predecessors presumably were.

The magnates leading the ceremony were the earls of Mentieth, Strathearn and, reflecting his hereditary duty as kingmaker, Fife. The latter two are depicted behind the clerics on the seal, their identities confirmed by their heraldic shields on either side of

43 *The southern edge of the Moot Hill at Scone.* Nick Aitchison

the royal arms below the king's feet. The earls of Strathearn and Fife are presumably the individuals on either side of Alexander in the illustration. At the cross, 'With due reverence they installed him there on the royal throne'. This was done 'in accordance with the custom which had grown up in the kingdom from antiquity'. The prominent roles accorded to these earls confirms the essentially regional character of the ritual and suggests its possible origins in the inauguration ceremony of the kings of Fortriu.

The 'royal seat of stone' was draped in gold-embroidered silk cloths. The Stone's role was traditional and fundamental. According to Fordun, 'no king was ever accustomed to reign in Scotland unless he had first, upon receiving the name of king, sat upon this stone at Scone'. Fordun adds that 'this stone is reverently kept in that same monastery for the consecration of the kings of Scots', implying that it was treated as a holy relic. The Stone, which must have been removed from the abbey church specifically for the ceremony, may have been housed in a wooden throne. The seal depicts the outline of a backless throne but, in the illustration, Alexander's robes obscure whatever he is sitting on.

Fordun states that the bishop of St Andrews then consecrated Alexander, but it seems more likely that Fordun mistakenly reversed the order of the 'blessing and ordination' with the enthronement. Alternatively, Fordun may have confused this with the next part of the ceremony, not described by Bower but illustrated on the seal. This shows two clerics, one mitred the other unmitred, presumably the bishop of St Andrews and abbot of Scone respectively. They are depicted adjusting Alexander's mantle, having just enrobed him 'in royal purple', as Bower records: the king still holds the fastening in his left hand. The illustration depicts Alexander in his ceremonial robes.

Above the bishop on the seal is another figure, probably the bishop of Dunkeld, offering a rectangular object in his outstretched hand. This is possibly a house-shrine for storing saints' relics, similar to the Monymusk reliquary (**44**). The bishop's presence reflects Dunkeld's former status as the head of the Celtic Church in Scotland, the resting place of the relics of St Columba after they were transferred from Iona in 849, and therefore provides a direct link with the Scots' cradle of Christianity, where Columba consecrated Aedán as king of Dál Riata in 574. The seal probably depicts the bishop presenting the reliquary to the king for him to swear an oath upholding the faith.

Bower then describes how 'the king was solemnly seated ... with his crown on his head and his sceptre in his hand'. Both seal and illustration depict Alexander wearing an open lily-crown. The seal shows a slender sceptre with a lily-shaped finial resting in the king's right hand, while the illustration depicts him holding a heavier sceptre with a foliated and bulbous terminal in his left hand. But there is no evidence that Alexander received either crown or sceptre during the inauguration ceremony. Although Bower refers to Alexander's coronation, this reflects his anachronistic perception of the ceremony; Fordun makes no reference to coronation. Although a St Andrews source of *c*.1255 claims that Alexander was crowned by the bishop of St Andrews, in 1251 the Scots again petitioned the pope for permission to crown and anoint their king, revealing that these had not featured in the inauguration of Alexander III in 1249. Alexander may have worn a crown, but coronation and anointment were not part of the ritual.

The nobles then set down their stools at the king's feet to listen to a sermon, according to Bower. But Fordun describes how 'the earls and other nobles, on bended knee, strewed their garments under his [Alexander's] feet, before the stone', in some form of ceremony of obeisance or fealty to the king. This may be the final element in the *Chronicle of Melrose*'s account of how Alexander was inaugurated 'in the ancestral manner on 13 July, made king by the magnates, placed on the paternal throne and honoured by all as lawful heir'.

Then a highlander (*Scotus montanus*), 'honourably attired after his own fashion, clad in a scarlet robe', blessed the king. Fordun and the illustration both record his words as 'Benach de Re Albanne', from the Gaelic *Beannachd Dhé, Rí Alban* ('The blessing of God, O King of Scotland'). The poet then recited the king's pedigree, in Gaelic, back through 56 generations to Fergus, the first King of Scots, and from him back to Hiber, the first Scot, and his parents, Gaidheal Glas and Scota. The king's pedigree appears to have been read from a document rather than recited from memory. While the illustration appears to show a medieval speech bubble, Fordun states that it was read and the seal depicts a figure, behind the abbot, holding a long and narrow object, possibly an unrolled parchment. The small figure depicted on the seal immediately behind the poet may be a harper to accompany him.

Although Fordun states that the king's genealogy was read *after* his inauguration, the prominence given to it in these descriptions and depictions attests its importance as an integral element of the ceremony. The king's genealogy confirmed his right to the kingship and, by reciting it at his inauguration, the poet was publicly proclaiming the king's title to rule. The importance of this role indicates that the highlander was the king's poet, a senior position in a hereditary bardic class. The poet was certainly perceived to have been of status by Bower's time, as he is portrayed wearing a sword. This illustration

44 *The Monymusk reliquary. Although now empty, this eighth-century casket would formerly have held the relics of a saint.* Copyright: The Trustees of the National Museums of Scotland

also strengthens the case that the king's pedigree was read or recited during the inauguration ceremony because it shows that the king has yet to receive the sword of state. The sword is held aloft by a noble, presumably the earl of Fife, standing to the right of the enthroned king. The earl is shown about to present the sword to the king, whose right hand remains free to accept it. This appears to have been the concluding act of the ceremony.

By 1249 the Scottish inauguration ritual comprised two halves. The first, probably conducted in the abbey church by Scotland's senior bishop and dominated by the king's 'blessing and ordination', was overtly ecclesiastical in nature. The second, performed outdoors and comprising the king's enthronement on the Stone or a throne containing it, some act of obeisance by the nobles, the recital of the king's genealogy and investiture with a sword and/or sceptre, was secular in character. The first stage of this composite ritual represents an ecclesiastical veneer, added to the ancient ceremony of enthronement on the Stone.

The identification of two discrete elements within Alexander III's inauguration enables the form of earlier ceremonies to be inferred. The inherently conservative nature of kingship and ritual and the use of the past as a source of legitimacy indicates that the ceremony's second part is closely related to earlier practices of royal inauguration. The traditional ritual was probably performed on the Moot Hill and its principal act comprised enthronement on the Stone, with or without an enclosing throne. Other elements may have included an act of fealty from the king's assembled subjects or nobles, although this may have been added after the introduction of feudalism to Scotland and originally may have comprised the public acclamation of the king. The recital of the king's genealogy appears to be an archaic and important feature. Although Alexander III was inaugurated in 1249, the ceremony's constituent elements provide a unique insight into the rituals by which early Scottish and perhaps Pictish kings were installed. Royal inauguration ceremonies clearly altered over time but drew extensively on the past and were presented and/or perceived as ancient and unchanging. In particular, the enthroning of the king on the Stone, celebrated on the Moot Hill, appears to be of great antiquity. Its origins may lie in Pictish and perhaps even pagan inauguration ritual.

The growing power of the Church, reflected in the foundation of Scone Priory in 1114, probably had a profound influence on inauguration ceremonies. A prominent ecclesiastical dimension to the ritual is evident from 1124, when unidentified bishops played a central role, and the bishop of St Andrews, Scotland's senior prelate, led the ceremony in 1214. By 1249, its influence had enabled the Church to prefix the traditional inauguration ceremony with an ecclesiastical ritual that gave Scotland's prelates a powerful role in the making of kings, rivalling that of the senior magnates in the second part of the ceremony. The Church did not supplant the archaic inauguration ritual but set it in a new, explicitly Christian, context.

The ceremony's changing nature and the Church's increasing influence are evident in the last Scottish inauguration to be held on the Stone. Emerging as the successful competitor from the Great Cause to determine the succession to the Scottish kingship, 'On the last day of November 1292, John de Balliol was made king at Scone; and raised up there on the royal throne, as was the custom', as Fordun describes. English accounts suggest that John's inauguration differed from those of his predecessors. Rishanger and Guisborough both record that John was enthroned 'on the royal stone', Guisborough adding that it was conducted 'in the Scottish manner' (*more Scottorum*). But both also state that this occurred *inside* the abbey church at Scone. Although Rishanger states that John was 'crowned ceremoniously', this reflects the influence of English rituals and the fact that he was writing some forty years after the event. In contrast, Guisborough uniquely describes John's enthronement as a 'substitute coronation' (*loco quasi coronacionis*); coronation was still not part of the ceremony.

Other differences reflect the political circumstances of Balliol's inauguration. Edward I authorised John de St John to install Balliol because the earl of Fife, who hereditarily performed this role, was still an infant. And the senior cleric who officiated was Anthony Bek, Bishop of Durham. That the ceremony was led by an English magnate and prelate emphasised Balliol's subjection to Edward. At Newcastle-Upon-Tyne on 26 December, Balliol did homage to Edward for his kingdom, acknowledging English overlordship of Scotland (**colour plate 17**).

The Scottish inauguration ritual contains rich layers of symbolism. The ceremony was conducted before, and with the approval of, the assembled nobility, representing the Scottish nation. The king was installed by the most senior bishops and earls of Scotland. The prelates conferred divine sanction, their role attesting the close links between kingship and Church. The hereditary roles of the earls of Fife and Strathearn as kingmakers ensured the support of two of Scotland's most powerful magnates and originated in their position as heads of collateral branches of the royal kin group which had been excluded from the kingship over two centuries before. The link with the past is expressed more explicitly in the recital of the royal pedigree, tracing the inauguree's lineage back through a long line of kings and his descent from the mythical ancestors of the Scots. These symbolic elements comprised a strategy of legitimation, demonstrating the inauguree's status as a righteous king and thereby projecting his kingship as unchallengeable, at least in theory.

STONES, THRONES AND MOUNDS

Some of the richest symbolism displayed by the Scottish, and before that possibly Pictish, inauguration ritual concerns its physical contexts, the Moot Hill, royal throne and, of course, the Stone of Destiny itself. Enthronement was the most distinctive element of the early Scottish inauguration ritual. But why were kings installed on a stone, which was probably housed in a throne on a mound? This section assesses the symbolic significance of the inauguration ceremony as revealed by these features and their parallels.

The Stone and the act of sitting on it embody a range of symbolic meanings. The physical properties of stone, its hardness and antiquity, give it a universal symbolism of stability and permanence: stones outlast kings. But there is nothing specifically pagan about this and it does not attest the 'worship' of stones. Moreover, the association of kings with stones is fully compatible with concepts of Christian kingship, as Biblical precedents such as the coronation of Joash (2 Kings 11.12–14) attest.

A rich vein of mythology links stones and king-making and attributes an oracular function to certain stones. Arthur famously drew the sword Excalibur from a stone as a test of his right to the kingship. The early Irish myth, *De Síl Chonairi Moir* (*Of the Descendants of Conaire Mór*), describes how aspiring kings of Tara had to undergo a series of initiatory tests. If the inauguree was the rightful king, two flagstones would part to let his chariot through and the *Lia Fáil* would screech against the chariot's axle. The Stone's oracular role is revealed by its prophecy, one translation of which refers to the noise emitted by the Stone, although this presumably reflects confusion with the *Lia Fáil*:

> Unless the fixed decrees of fate give way,
> The Scots shall govern and the sceptre sway
> Where'er this stone they find, and its dread sound obey.

The antiquity of inauguration rituals involving stones in Scotland is suggested by several carved footprints, singly or in pairs, although their date is unknown (**45**). The kings of Dál Riata may have been inaugurated in a (shoed) footprint carved into the bedrock within the early medieval hillfort of Dunadd, mid-Argyll (**46**). Its ritual associations may be supported by a boar, basin, and ogam inscription carved beside the footprint (**47**). The significance of carved footprints is revealed by accounts of inauguration ceremonies in Elizabethan Ireland and those practised by the Lords of the Isles during the seventeenth century. Edmund Spenser's *A View of the State of Ireland* (1595) records that:

> They use to place him that shal be their Captain upon a stone always reserved for that purpose, and placed commonly upon a hill; in some of which I have seen formed and engraven a foot, which they say was the measure of their first Captain's foot, whereon he, standing, receives an oath to preserve all the ancient former customs of the country inviolable.

1 *Clickhimin, Shetland: one of the most important broch excavations of the twentieth century*

2 *Mousa, Shetland: the archetypal broch tower*

3 *Dun Cuier, Barra*

4 *Dun Carloway, Lewis: the partial collapse of the broch tower reveals the inner structure of the walls*

5 *Loch na Beirgh broch tower, Lewis: before excavation this structure was visible only as a low mound in a boggy field*

6 *Clickhimin: the blockhouse, seen from the ruins of the broch tower walls*

7 *Dun Telve, Glenelg: the detail of the wall construction can clearly be seen where parts of the wall have fallen away*

8 *Dun Telve: the interior wall displays the familiar features of broch architecture*

9 *The broch tower of Mousa dominates the small island. This view shows the island of Mousa from mainland Shetland. The broch tower is visible between the two central telegraph poles on the near horizon*

10 *Dun Dornaigil, Sutherland: a detail of the distinctive triangular lintel over the entrance*

11 *Carn Liath, Caithness: a view out through the entrance showing the checks for the wooden door*

12 *Mousa: a view looking up the internal stairs*

13 *Dun Carloway in its landscape context*

14 *Dun Beag, Skye in its landscape*

15 *Dun Loch Druim an Iasgair, Benbecula: an Atlantic roundhouse set on an inaccessible islet, typical of many in the Hebrides*

16 *Dun na Kille, Barra: built into the corner of a modern cemetery, this well-preserved Atlantic roundhouse escaped detection until quite recently*

17 *Gurness, Orkney: the internal stone furniture*

18 *Dun Cuier, Barra: although the interior of this complex roundhouse is clogged with rubble, the scarcement ledge is clearly visible*

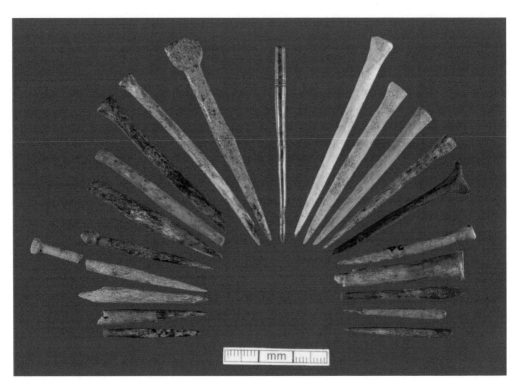

19 *Typical finds: a selection of bone pins from the broch tower at Loch na Beirgh, Lewis*

20 *Dun Telve seen from neighbouring Dun Troddan*

21 *An iron spade-shoe from Cnip wheelhouse in Lewis, dating to the first century AD. The spade rather than the plough was the main cultivation implement in the area until recent centuries. A similar one was recovered from the southern broch of Leckie in Stirlingshire*

22 *Gurness, Orkney: the archetypal broch village*

23 *Jarlshof, Shetland, from the air: the broch tower forms part of a long-lived settlement from the Bronze Age to the medieval period*

45 *The carved pair of footprints, faintly visible in the centre of the large flagstone, at Clickhimin, Shetland.* Copyright: Royal Commission on the Ancient and Historical Monuments of Scotland

By stepping into the footprint, the inauguree was literally following in the steps of his ancestors, an explicit demonstration of the ruling dynasty's continuity and therefore the legitimacy of his kingship. But the king was also symbolically connecting himself with the land, his kingdom, reflecting the archaic sacral role of kings as guarantors of their kingdom's fertility and attesting his status as a righteous king.

Thrones performed a similar function to stones, providing an object on which the king may be ritually installed. Indeed, the distinction between stones and thrones is sometimes blurred. The Stone may have been held within the Scottish throne, although it is unclear if it was kept there permanently or only for inaugurations. This may attest an evolution from installation directly on the Stone to enthronement on a wooden throne incorporating the Stone. The adoption of thrones may have been influenced by bishops' cathedra. These were sometimes of stone, such as the rather plain but impressive St Wilfrid's Chair, or Frid Stool, in Hexham Abbey, Northumberland. It was probably from ecclesiastical exemplars that Charlemagne's great but unornamented throne of white marble, raised on five steps in Aachen Cathedral, was derived.

More 'primitive' thrones were still used after the Middle Ages in some areas. Irish kings were 'placed with certain barbarous ceremonies on a seat of stone, in the open air, on some hill', according to William Camden's *Britannia* (1586). A surviving example, the inauguration chair of the Clandeboye O'Neills of Castlereagh, is crudely hewn from a single sandstone block (**48**), while the O'Neill Earls of Tyrone were installed at Tullaghoge in a stone chair formed from several slabs (**colour plate 18**; **49**). Although similar in form, the throne of the medieval dukes of Carinthia at Zollfeld in Austria was constructed

46 *The carved footprint (bottom right) and ogam inscription, using natural flaws in the rock as a baseline, at Dunadd, mid-Argyll.* Copyright: Royal Commission on the Ancient and Historical Monuments of Scotland

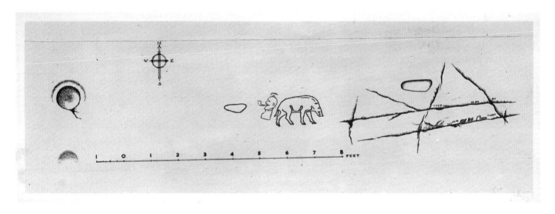

47 *The inscribed rock surface near the summit of the early medieval hillfort at Dunadd, mid-Argyll. In addition to one hollowed and one pecked-out footprint, an incised boar, an ogam inscription and basin distinguish this as an important location, probably with ritual associations. The crudely carved portrait of a character smoking a pipe is a modern addition.* Copyright: Royal Commission on the Ancient and Historical Monuments of Scotland

48 *The inauguration chair of the Clandeboye O'Neills. Originally from Castlereagh near Belfast, it is now in the Ulster Museum.* Photograph reproduced with the kind permission of the Trustees of the National Museums and Galleries of Northern Ireland

from Roman masonry (**50**), drawing on the legitimacy conferred by an imperial past.

The ritual seating of kings on a stone or throne also echoes practices of sacral kingship and is ultimately derived from a primitive Indo-European ceremony in which couples were married by sitting down together. Here enthronement symbolises the ritual marriage of king and kingdom. When reduced to its underlying symbolism, the early Scottish inauguration ceremony has more in common with the primitive ritual reported by Giraldus than initially apparent. This symbolism emphasises that the Stone was not originally of importance in its own right. Instead it was the act of enthronement rather than the stone or throne on which the inauguree was installed that was significant. The Stone used may simply have been one of suitable size and shape and only over time and through its close association with kings and their inauguration did the Stone gradually acquire its symbolic significance.

Fertility symbolism is also suggested by the location of several inauguration places. Scone, Dunadd (**51**), and Kingston-upon-Thames, where the West Saxon kings were supposedly crowned on a large sandstone block (**colour plate 19**); all lie at the highest tidal reach of the rivers Tay, Add and Thames respectively. This is a symbolically significant location 'where the salt waters of the sea (and the powers of death who dwell in it) are finally turned back by the living waters of the river', as Professor Archie Duncan notes. In a late expression of the association between inauguration place and fertility, Robert III (1390–1406) attended a harvest festival at Scone. But Scone is also associated

49 *The coronation chair of the dukes of Carinthia at Zollfell, Austria, constructed from reused Roman masonry*

with death. The *Prophecy of Berchán* foretold that Macbeth would be slain at Scone and this was where the Pictish nobility was reputedly slaughtered. In an age when a contested throne was settled only with the death of the incumbent or the challenger, the inauguration centre was perceived to be where kingship (and life) was lost as well as conferred.

Early Scottish and possibly Pictish kings were inaugurated on the Moot Hill at Scone. This is a flat-topped mound, oval in plan and approximately 328 x 230ft (100 x 70m) across and 10ft (3m) high (**37, 42, 43**). Despite persistent claims, there is no evidence that it is a prehistoric burial mound, although the presence of prehistoric ritual monuments nearby is suggestive. More probably, it was either purpose-built or modelled from a natural feature. Only excavation, or perhaps geophysical survey, can reveal its origins and construction.

The Moot Hill was the focus of royal activities at Scone from at least 906 when Constantine and Cellach made their proclamation on the 'Hill of Faith' (*collis credulitatis*). This is almost certainly 'the Moot Hill on which stood the royal seat at Scone where the kings sitting on the throne in royal attire are accustomed to proclaim judgements, laws and statutes to their subjects'. Although mentioned within the context of Malcolm II's reign (1005–34), Fordun was referring to a widespread practice that was perceived to be of some antiquity. The throne referred to was probably the throne on which Scottish kings were installed, although it may not have housed the Stone permanently. The Stone was kept in the abbey church in 1249, according to Fordun, and may only have been removed specifically for inauguration ceremonies. The throne, in contrast, may have been used for a wider range of royal business, although it too may not have been a permanent fixture on the Moot Hill.

50 *The inauguration of an O'Neill on the stone chair at Tullaghoge, Co. Tyrone. The figure on the right casts a shoe over O'Neill's head, symbolising that the new O'Neill should continue to walk in the footsteps of his predecessors. A detail from the Map of Ulster by Richard Bartlett or his school, 1602.* B9676/7. Copyright: National Maritime Museum, Greenwich

51 *The early medieval hillfort at Dunadd, mid-Argyll, from the air. The meandering River Add and its oxbows, fossilising the river's earlier courses, are clearly visible.* Dr Stephen Driscoll

The Moot Hill retained is significance after the Stone's removal in 1296. In 1371, Robert II convened a parliament the day after his coronation, 'the king sitting, as use is, in the royal seat, upon the Mount of Scone', according to the *Acts of the Parliaments of Scotland*. In 1390, Robert III also held a parliament 'upon the Mount of Scone on the north side of the monastery beyond the cemetery', which has led to its identification with the Moot Hill being challenged. But the existing burial ground at Scone post-dates the Reformation, judging from its gravestones, while burials found during the nineteenth century reveal that the medieval cemetery lay further west, placing the Moot Hill to its north, consistent with this source (**37**). Given its enduring royal associations, it must have been on the Moot Hill, the only recorded mound at Scone, that Alexander III was enthroned in 1249 (**colour plate 16**). The Moot Hill was known as *Montem Placiti*, the 'Hill of Pleas', according to Sir John Skene's *Regiam Majestatem* (1609), because courts of justice were still held on it.

The Moot Hill performed both practical and symbolic functions. Like a throne, it raised the king above his assembled subjects, expressing his superior, literally elevated, status. Its flat top also formed an extensive stage, enabling the ritual theatre of the inauguration ceremony to be viewed. This spectacle was intended to impress, emphasising the social distance between the king and his subjects. This was part of a wider strategy for legitimising the inauguree's kingship and rendering him less open to challenge.

The Moot Hill's identification as the inauguration place at Scone is also supported by parallels. Medieval assembly places and popular courts were often held at mounds of various type. Excavation reveals that Secklow Hundred Mound, Buckinghamshire, was probably constructed in the tenth century, while a medieval regality court at Coupar Angus met on a Bronze Age kerbed cairn. Some mounds have expressly royal associations, as St Andrews' earlier names, *Cennrígmonad* and *Cellrígmonad* ('headland/church of the mound of kings'), attest. In particular, the Moot Hill belongs to a wider pattern of medieval rituals of royalty. Mounds are an integral component of many Irish royal centres. And of 29 confirmed and 26 possible inauguration sites in Ireland there are mounds at ten and five respectively. Some mounds may have been associated with inauguration thrones and/or stones; the uneven form of the Clandeboye O'Neills' chair suggests that it was originally set in an earthen mound. Although widely assumed to be prehistoric funerary monuments, many Irish inauguration mounds were probably purpose-built. Indeed, Old Irish *forrad* describes a flat-topped turf mound constructed for various functions, including inauguration ceremonies. Nevertheless, the Mound of the Hostages (*Dumha na nGiall*) at Tara, on which the *Lia Fáil* once stood, is a Neolithic passage tomb dating to around 3000 BC (**3**).

The presence of earlier burial mounds at medieval royal centres attests their appropriation and investment with ideological meaning by socio-political élites. The association of kings with ancient funerary monuments is laden with symbolism. By awarding themselves an auspicious but mythical ancestry, kings were drawing on the legitimacy conferred by the past, projecting themselves as righteous rulers and, therefore, as unchallengeable. Burial mounds were a physical expression of the king's genealogical origins, paralleling the reading of the king's genealogy at the inauguration of Alexander III.

The *Book of Lecan*, an early fifteenth-century compilation of earlier Irish texts, stresses the importance of a king's inauguration on the cairn in which the founder of the royal dynasty is claimed to be buried. This describes the inauguration of the Ó Dubhda (O'Dowd) kings of *Tír nAmalgado* (Tirawley), Co Mayo:

> should Ó Dubhda happen to be in *Tír nAmalgado* he may repair to *Carn nAmalgado* to be nominated, so as that all the chiefs are about him ... for it was Amalgaid mac Fiachra Algaidh who raised that cairn for himself, in order that he himself, and all those who should obtain the lordship after him, might receive the style of lord upon it. And it is in this cairn that Amalgaid himself is interred, and it is from him it is named. And every king of the race of Fiachra that shall not be thus nominated, he shall have shortness of life, and his race or generations shall not be illustrious, and he shall never see the kingdom of God.

Although the Stone and the Moot Hill are the best known examples of their type, they belong to a wider pattern of royal rituals in Scotland and Ireland, with echoes in central and western Europe. Stones, thrones and mounds were important elements in the strategies of legitimation employed by medieval kings.

COSMOLOGICAL SYMBOLISM

Medieval cosmology was élite knowledge and a vehicle for disseminating ideology; by promoting their own view of the world's origins and organisation, ruling élites could legitimise their own privileged place within it. The universal cosmological concepts of concern here are the *axis mundi* (world axis) and *imago mundi* (world image). The *axis mundi* is perceived to link the planes of existence, such as heaven, earth and hell, and is widely symbolised by an upright and/or elevated feature, often a tower, tree or mountain, and located at the centre of a building, town, country or continent. This is where cosmological powers are believed to enter the world and flow across the landscape towards the cardinal points, making it a place of great spiritual and symbolic significance. The centre symbolises the whole, symbolically reproducing the wider unit to which it belongs, thereby forming an *imago mundi*. This concept is attested in an eleventh-century reference to the 'kingdom of Scone'.

The Stone, the Moot Hill and Scone all exhibit cosmological symbolism. Fordun remarks that the Stone 'was kept carefully in its own particular place to be, as it were, an anchor'. Felix Skene's translation, that the Scots kept the Stone 'as the anchor of their national existence', reinforces this, as does *Liber Extravagans*' reference to the Stone as the 'anchor of life' (*anchora vite*). These sources express the Stone's symbolic role as the *axis mundi* securing Scone and, indeed, the kingdom of the Scots within the cosmos.

The Moot Hill is rich with cosmological symbolism and represents a physical expression of both the *axis mundi* and *imago mundi*. That the early Scottish kings were drawing on the cosmological powers associated with the *axis mundi* is apparent from their inauguration on the Moot Hill and the exercise of their legislative and judicial roles there. The Moot Hill's status as an *imago mundi* is expressed in the tradition, related by Fordun, that 'Malcolm [II] was so lavish or rather wasteful in gifts that, although he had held all the lands, regions and provinces of the whole kingdom in his own possession in the ancient manner, he kept hold of none of it for himself apart from the Moot Hill on which stood the royal seat of Scone'. This is unlikely, but it is the underlying symbolism that is important: the Moot Hill symbolised the kingdom and its retention therefore symbolised Malcolm's authority over all Scotland. His kingship was perceived to depend on the possession of the Moot Hill alone.

The Moot Hill's perception as an *imago mundi* is confirmed by the traditions and alternative names attached to it. One name, *Omnis Terra* ('the whole of the land'), epitomises the very concept of the *imago mundi*. Sir John Skene's *Regiam Majestatem* (1609) attributes the name's origin to the practice of barons bringing some earth with them when they gave homage to the king at Scone. Over time, the soil accumulated to form the Moot Hill. The Moot Hill, perceived to comprise part of every Scottish barony, symbolised all Scotland and the king's presence on it symbolised his rule over his entire kingdom. According to J. Morison's *Sconiana* (1807), 'It was a proverbial saying, even within these [last] few years, that when a person walked over the Mote-hill, he had walked over all Scottish land'. Although merely a corruption of Moot Hill, another of the mound's names, Boot Hill, is traditionally attributed to the practice of Scottish nobles placing earth from their lands inside their boots before swearing fealty to the king, the emptied earth supposedly forming Boot Hill. Although these traditions are of doubtful historical veracity, they express cosmological concepts and this symbolism enables their historical significance to be appreciated.

As the royal inauguration place and pre-eminent royal centre, Scone symbolised the *axis mundi* and may have been the focus of a wider cosmological scheme. William Skene suggested that the province of Gowrie, within which Scone is located, was formed from the adjacent parts of four Pictish provinces south of the Grampian Mountains. The twelfth-century *De Situ Albanie* records these as Angus with the Mearns, Atholl (which it pairs with Gowrie), Fife with Fothrif, and Strathearn with Menteith. Irish versions of Nennius' *Historia Brittonum* give what appear to be earlier, unitary names for the same provinces: *Cirich* (recorded elsewhere as *Circen*), *Fotla*, *Fib* and *Fortrenn* (*Fortriu*). Skene interpreted Gowrie's creation from its surrounding provinces as the acquisition of mensal lands by the kingship, based at Scone. But this is actually a cosmological arrangement of peripheral provinces around a central, superior province (**52**), a well-known phenomenon in early medieval Ireland. Emphasising Scone's importance, the central province, in which the principal royal centre is located, is closely associated with the kingship in such schemes. Scone may lie at the centre of a cosmological scheme embracing southern Pictland and/or *Alba*, the embryonic kingdom of the Scots, making it unclear whether this is Pictish or Scottish in origin.

Despite the fragmentary evidence, it is clear that Scone, its Moot Hill, throne and Stone all performed symbolic and functional roles of fundamental importance to the early Scottish kingship, and probably the Pictish kingship before that. It was around the Moot Hill at Scone that the major affairs of state – royal inaugurations, assemblies, parliaments and courts – revolved. The Moot Hill was the symbolic centre of the kingdom of the Scots.

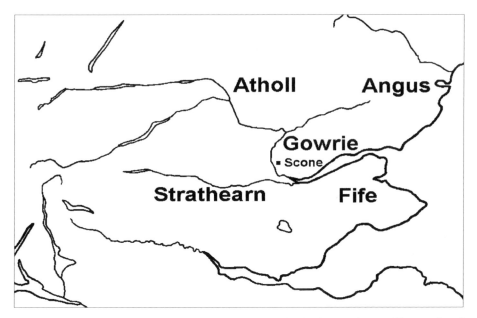

52 *Scone and its adjacent provinces. Eastern central Scotland, showing the possible cosmological arrangement of Scone as the* axis mundi, *within the central province of Gowrie and surrounded by peripheral provinces.* Nick Aitchison

SCONE AFTER THE STONE

Scone's importance did not diminish after the Stone of Destiny was removed by Edward I in 1296. Indeed, Scone's status as the inauguration place of the Scottish kings ensured that it was the setting of some of the most momentous events of the Scottish War of Independence and a focus of opposition during even the darkest days of English domination. As soon as Edward withdrew from Scotland, Scottish magnates held a parliament at Scone at which twelve Guardians of the Realm were appointed 'to guard and defend the freedom of the kingdom' and its people, as Fordun records. But in a symbolic expression of the Scots' conquest, William Ormsby, Edward's appointee as Justiciar of Scotland, held his court at Scone in May 1297. Two Guardians, Sir William Wallace and Sir William Douglas, led a Scottish attack on Scone. Although Ormsby escaped, much English booty was taken and the action ignited a popular rising against English rule. It was Scone's royal associations and its abbot's support for the cause of Scottish independence that prompted the English to sack the abbey in 1298. This was not, as some have claimed, a result of Edward looking for the 'real' Stone, having realised that the stone he had seized in 1296 was a substitute.

Another notable event was also one of the most famous inaugurations to be celebrated at Scone, and the first since the Stone was seized. After his ambitions on the Scottish kingship were revealed to Edward, Robert Bruce, Earl of Carrick, fled from London to Dumfries, where he killed his betrayer, Sir John ('the Red') Comyn. Robert, a grandson of a competitor in the Great Cause, then demanded recognition as King of Scots from Edward. Fordun records that 'Robert Bruce ... hastened to Scone, taking with him as many [supporters] as he could, and on 27 March 1306, sitting on the royal seat, he was crowned in the fashion in which the kings of Scotland were customarily distinguished'. Robert's contested kingship and his precarious political and military position made the legitimacy bestowed by a traditional inauguration ceremony all the more important. However, by then the earl of Fife, the hereditary inaugurator of Scottish kings, was dead so his sister, Isabel, Countess of Buchan, performed the ceremony. An outraged Edward complained to the pope that Scone Abbey was 'placed in the midst of a perverse nation' and should be removed to a 'safer' place.

Scone's continued status as a royal centre throughout the fourteenth century and into the fifteenth is attested by the affairs of state conducted there, including parliaments, signing of royal charters and making of kings. But kings were not still inaugurated as Alexander III was in 1249. The Scots reaffirmed their independence with Robert's victory at the Battle of Bannockburn in 1314, but the ritual of anointment still eluded their kings. Robert petitioned the pope for the right to coronation and anointing and these were eventually conferred in a papal bull issued on 13 June 1329. This came too late for Robert, who had died six days earlier. His son David was only five years old but, at Scone in 1331, became the first Scottish king to be crowned and anointed, in a ceremony performed by the bishop of St Andrews. No longer could Scottish kings be considered inferior to their English counterparts.

Reflecting its continued status as the inauguration place of the kings of Scots, Scone remained a strategic objective during the second Scottish War of Independence. Seizing the opportunity presented by David II's minority, Edward Balliol, son of King John, invaded Scotland in 1332 with a force of Scottish and English nobles whose Scottish estates had been forfeited by Robert. After defeating a superior Scottish force at Dupplin Moor near Perth, they advanced on their strategic objective, Scone, where Edward was crowned by the earl of Fife and bishop of Dunkeld.

Over the next century every Scottish king was crowned at Scone; Robert II in 1371, Robert III in 1390, and James I in 1424. Scone continued to be the focus of elaborate sequences of royal rituals. Robert II was buried, 'in royal fashion' according to Bower, at Scone on 14 August 1390; Robert III was crowned by the bishop of St Andrews the following day and his queen, Anabella, was crowned by the bishop of Dunkeld the day after that. The desire to avoid an interregnum was still strong.

But the ancient royal centre was beginning to fall from favour, eclipsed by the more popular urban centres of Perth, Stirling and Edinburgh. Scone's long, slow decline is attested by the number of parliaments held and royal charters signed there. The last parliament held at Scone was in 1401 and although James I was crowned there in 1424, the ensuing parliament was held at Perth. After 1424, Scottish kings were crowned not at an appointed place but usually at Edinburgh or Stirling. Scone's abandonment as the coronation place of the Scottish kings may also reflect royal sensitivities; James II was crowned at Holyrood Abbey, possibly because Scone was near Perth, where his father was murdered. But James I was not the last king of Scots to be crowned at Scone. While Cromwellian forces occupied England, Ireland and Scotland south of the Forth, Charles II was crowned king of Scots by the Marquis of Argyll on 1 January 1651. Once again, a king was seeking the legitimacy derived from the ancient inauguration place of the Scottish

53 *The memorial to Sir David Murray of Gospetrie, First Lord Scone and Viscount Stormont, within the Stormont Mausoleum on the Moot Hill at Scone.* Copyright: Royal Commission on the Ancient and Historical Monuments of Scotland

54 *'The Prospect of the House and Town of Skuyn', as engraved by D. John Slezer in* Theatrum Scotiae *(1693). Viewed from the south, Scone Palace is in the centre, while the* toun *stretches along a single street (right).* Copyright: Royal Commission on the Ancient and Historical Monuments of Scotland

55 *Scone Palace from the north, as engraved by A. Rutherford in 1775, before it was rebuilt in Gothic style.* Copyright: Royal Commission on the Ancient and Historical Monuments of Scotland

kings. But Charles suffered multiple indignities; he was crowned on a improvised wooden dais inside the church, made to resubscribe to the Scottish Covenants and subjected to a 90-minute sermon on political absolutism.

Although Scone never witnessed another coronation, it continued to draw royal visitors. Scone's symbolic significance attracted the claimants to the throne during both Jacobite rebellions. Prince James Francis Edward Stewart ('The Old Pretender') made his base there during the 1715 rising, where he prepared for his coronation but was forced to withdraw before it could be held. Prince Charles Edward Stewart ('Bonnie Prince Charlie' or 'The Young Pretender') visited Scone during the 1745 Jacobite rebellion. Later royal visits were in very different circumstances. Queen Victoria visited Scone in 1842, recording in her *Leaves from the Journal of our Life in the Highlands* that she and Prince Albert 'saw the mound on which the ancient Scotch kings were always crowned'.

Despite its declining royal associations, Scone was still an important ecclesiastical and pilgrimage centre. At least some of the *Scone Antiphonary*, including a 19-part mass, was composed by Robert Carver, an early sixteenth-century canon of Scone. Scone Abbey survived until the Reformation, although its community then numbered only about sixteen canons. In 1559, the abbey, church and abbot's palace were destroyed by a mob from Perth, incited by a speech by John Knox. Knox's *Historie of the Reformation* (1587) describes how 'The Multitude easelie inflamed, gave the Allarm: And so was that Abbay and Plaice apointed to Sackage; in doing quhairof they tuk no lang Deliberatioun, bot comitted the holle to the Merciment of Fyre'.

Scone's first commendator after the Reformation, the earl of Gowrie, began rebuilding the palace but his lands were forfeited by the Crown in 1600. In 1604, James VI granted the lands of Scone abbey to Sir David Murray of Gospetrie and made him the first Lord Scone in 1605. Murray completed the reconstruction. John Monipennie's *A True Description and Division of the Whole Realme of Scotland* (1612) noted that 'This Abbey was sumptuously builded, now wholly decayed: a part whereof is reedified, and pleasantly repaired by the Lord of Scone, being his speciall residence'. Murray removed the last upstanding remains of the abbey church and by 1624 had built a new church on top of the Moot Hill (**colour plate 20**). Murray died in 1631; his elaborate memorial dominates the interior of his church, now the Stormont Mausoleum (**53**). John Slezer's *Theatrum Scotiae* depicted the house, its policies and adjacent toun in 1693 (**54**).

By the 1770s, Scone Palace had fallen into disrepair (**55**). David, Seventh Viscount Stormont and later Second Earl of Mansfield, renovated the palace and it was inhabitable by 1783. The architect was George Paterson, although his plans were not fully adopted. The landscape gardener, Thomas White, was contracted to 'beautify all the uneven Ground near the Palace of Scone' and 'Cover the surface of the said Ground with good Earth', suggesting that underlying archaeological deposits may survive intact. The third earl succeeded his father in 1796 and in 1803 began rebuilding the palace and Stormont Mausoleum in asymmetrical neo-Gothic style and redesigning the policies. William Atkinson was the architect on this occasion and John Loudon the landscape gardener. The palace was inhabitable by 1808, with most work completed by 1812 (**colour plate 13; 56**). The third earl also removed the

56 *Scone Palace, the south-east front.* Nick Aitchison

adjacent village of Scone, which had occupied the site since medieval times, resettling its inhabitants at New Scone, 1.2 miles (2km) to the south-east.

There is little to suggest Scone's former status as a royal centre, although excavation may be productive. Scone's only visible link with its royal past is the Moot Hill.

6

THE STONE AT WESTMINSTER

a priceless treasure ... of which Westminster Abbey is a fitting casket.
Mrs G. A. Rogers, *The Coronation Chair and England's Interest In It* (1881)

The Stone of Destiny is intimately associated with Scone but has spent almost all its recorded history at Westminster. Although there has long been a tendency to study the Stone from a specifically Scottish perspective, its history at Westminster is as important as it is long. No account of the Stone would be complete without looking at how and why it came to be in Westminster Abbey, its historic role and symbolic significance there, and the peculiarly English myths and literary associations that the Stone's presence have generated. This long episode in the Stone's history was initiated by Edward I.

EDWARD I AND THE STONE

Edward I was aware of the nature of the Scottish royal inauguration ritual and exploited the differences between it and both English and continental practices. While English kings pressured the pope into refusing Scottish kings the right to be crowned and anointed, Edward used the absence of coronation and anointing from the Scottish inauguration ceremony to challenge the independent status of the Scottish kings. Edward also linked this with the issue of homage. In 1278, Alexander III acknowledged that he owed homage to Edward for his lands in England. But Edward claimed, unsuccessfully, that Scottish kings also owed homage to those of England for the kingdom of Scotland itself and ominously announced that he reserved the right to reopen the matter at a later date. The importance Edward attached to the Scottish king-making ceremony is apparent from his submissions to the Paris lawyers he consulted during the Great Cause. Edward's evidence began with the statement that 'The king of a certain kingdom [Scotland] was neither anointed nor crowned, but placed in a customary royal seat by the earls, magnates and prelates of the kingdom'. Edward clearly knew about the Stone and its significance.

After the English victory at Dunbar on 27 April 1296, the Scots capitulated and the rest of Edward's campaign that year was essentially a triumphal march around Scotland. Edward was in Perth on 21-25 June, where he celebrated St John's Day, the feast day of the city's patron saint. Although it is unclear if Edward visited Scone – only 1.5 miles (2.5km) north of Perth – on this occasion he must at least have passed the inauguration place on his way north. John Balliol, King of Scots, escaped with his life but not his dignity. At Montrose, sometime between 7 and 11 July, he was made to confess his errors and surrender the kingdom and people of Scotland to Edward. Balliol was then publicly humiliated by being stripped of his crown, sceptre and ring, while the royal arms and ermine were unceremoniously ripped from his surcoat, earning him the nickname 'Toom Tabard' ('Bare or Empty Surcoat') and everlasting disgrace (**colour plate 3**). Edward then proceeded as far north as Elgin; Balliol was sent south to imprisonment in the Tower of London.

Edward was back in Perth on 8 August when the Stone was seized. Rishanger records that 'In returning, he [Edward] passed by the Abbey of Scone, where having taken away the stone which the kings of Scots were accustomed at the time of their coronation to use for a throne, carried it to Westminster'. Little is known of the circumstances of the Stone's removal from Scone, but Guisborough implies that Edward himself visited Scone and personally commanded the Stone's possession: 'in returning by Scone [Edward] ordered that stone in which ... the kings of Scots were accustomed to be placed at their coronation, to be taken and carried to London'.

Blind Harry's *Wallace* (composed *c*.1476–78) claims that Edward was crowned king of Scots on the Stone at Scone, although this is uncorroborated:

> King Eduuard past and Cospatrick to Scwne
> And thar he gat homage of Scotland swne,
> For nane was left the Realme for to defend.
> For Ihon the Balyoune to Munros than he send
> And putt hym doune for euir of this kynrik.
> Than Eduuarde self was callit a Roy full ryk.
> The croune he tuk apon that sammyne stane.
> *(King Edward and Corspatrick marched to Scone*
> *And there he took homage of Scotland soon,*
> *For none were left, the kingdom to defend.*
> *Then for John Balliol to Montrose he sent*
> *And stripped him for ever of his kingship.*
> *Then Edward himself was called a rightful king.*
> *The crown he took upon that self-same stone.)*

Guisborough clearly states Edward's motives in seizing the Stone and transporting it to London, 'as a sign that the kingdom [of the Scots] had been conquered and resigned'. The Scots were fully aware of the symbolism, as Blind Harry reveals:

> This Iowell he gert turs in-till Ingland,
> In Lwnd it sett til witnes of this thing,
> Be conquest than of Scotland cald hym king.
> *(This jewel he then took into England,*
> *In London it sat, as witness of this thing,*
> *By conquering Scotland, they called him king.)*

It is unclear when this became an English objective. That the Stone was seized on the homeward leg need not reveal it as an afterthought; Edward's army was unlikely to take the Stone as far as the Moray coast only to have to carry it south again. There is no evidence that Scone in general, or the Stone in particular, were thought to be at risk from the English army or, despite persistent claims, of any warning to that effect. No assumptions concerning the Stone's authenticity can be made from the monks' failure to hide it. The (presumably wooden) throne that may have held the Stone was probably either left at Scone or destroyed. Although several seventeenth- and eighteenth-century English sources claim that Edward captured the chair on which the Scottish kings were inaugurated and took it to Westminster, they make the now familiar mistake of confusing the Stone with the chair that once held it or simply reflect the Stone's traditional description as a Chair.

From Perth, Edward took a circuitous route around Fife, travelling via St Andrews, Dunfermline and on to Stirling. The Stone either went with him or was taken directly to Stirling and on to Edinburgh. Edward's Wardrobe Accounts of 1303–04 record that 'a great Stone upon which the Kings of Scotland are [sic] accustomed to be crowned' was 'found' in Edinburgh Castle in 1297; the Stone evidently remained after Edward, who spent 17-18 August 1296 there, had left.

The Scottish regalia suffered a similar fate. In Edinburgh Castle, Edward's forces seized the crown, sceptre, sword of state, ring and robes; the 'other insignia of the kingdom of Scotland, carried with him [Edward] by violence to England', as Bisset records. Edward also took three coffers of jewellery and silver plate. Even religious relics were not spared. The Black Rood (cross) of St Margaret, a reliquary which was believed to contain a fragment of the True Cross on which Christ died, was taken. Some contemporary doggerel celebrating Edward's victories, incorporated in the *Chronicle* of Pierre Langtoft, refers to other relics:

In toune herd I telle,	*In [London] town I heard I tell,*
Thair baghel and thair belle	*their [the Scots'] staff and their bell*
ben filched and fledde.	*are stolen and fled.*

The 'baghel' and 'belle' are a pastoral staff (Gaelic, *bachall*) and square hammered bell, relics of Celtic saints which may also have been plundered from Scone.

That regalia and relics, which were more portable and easily concealed than the Stone, fell into English hands suggests that the Scots made no attempt to hide them. The Scots may not have suspected them to be at risk. Edward was waging a cultural warfare that he had developed during his conquest of Wales. In 1284 he acquired 'that part of the most holy wood of the cross which is called by the Welsh "Croysseneyht", which Llywelyn son of Griffin, late Prince of Wales, and his ancestors, princes of Wales, owned'. Edward is also said to have been presented with what was claimed to be King Arthur's crown. But the Scots, unfamiliar with Edward's methods of war, were unprepared. One Scottish crown temporarily eluded Edward's grasp, but was found in Balliol's baggage at Dover in 1299 as he was leaving for exile in Burgundy. This crown was given to Canterbury Cathedral. Not surprisingly, no early Scottish regalia has survived.

Edward used his spoils in an overtly political manner. Robert Wishart, Bishop of Glasgow, was made to swear fealty to Edward on both the Scottish and Welsh fragments of the True Cross. The Stone was used in a similar manner; it was more that a war trophy, but a symbol of Edward's conquest of Scotland. Edward did not take the Stone because it was a sacred relic: the tradition of it as Jacob's Pillow post-dates its arrival at Westminster. Instead, Edward's motives were political: he removed the Stone to demonstrate that he was now the overlord of Scotland and that in future the Scots were to have no other kings but Edward and his descendants. Edward believed that without the Stone on which its kings were installed, Scotland had ceased to be an independent sovereign nation, leaving England not only the dominant but the *only* kingdom within the British Isles.

In case Edward's claims of English superiority over Scotland and its kings were ever contested, he destroyed or removed large quantities of Scottish records. Scottish counter-arguments, closely related to the *Instructiones*, were reported to Edward: 'you have removed by force the muniments and writings and chronicles that they had in Scotland, in order to deprive them of defence and of evidence of the truth'. An inventory records that 65 boxes of Scottish documents, probably from Edinburgh Castle and Scone Abbey, were still in English hands in 1323. Edward's objective was to seize or destroy any artefact or document relating to Scotland's past or its kingship, to erase any sense of Scotland as an independent sovereign nation. The taking of the Stone symbolised that Scotland belonged to Edward.

Edward travelled to Westminster indirectly, arriving in June 1297. The Stone followed overland, as Langtoft's *Chronicle* describes:

Thair kinges sette of Scone   *Their [the Scots'] king's seat of Scone*
Es driven over done,   *Is driven over down,*
To Lunden i-ledde.   *and led to London.*

On 18 June 1297, Edward 'offered to the blessed King Edward [the Confessor], through whose virtues he had acquired them, the regalia of the Scottish kingdom; namely, the throne, golden sceptre and crown', as Matthew of Westminster records. The Stone, regalia and Black Rood were placed in the chapel in Westminster Abbey, dominated by St Edward the Confessor's shrine (**colour plates 21, 22**). Presenting the Stone and Scottish regalia to St Edward was, for Edward I, an act of both piety to his and England's patron saint and filial loyalty towards his father, Henry III, who had ordered the rebuilding of Westminster Abbey in 1241. The tombs of both Edward's father and queen, Eleanor of Castile, were within St Edward's Chapel, where Edward himself was to be buried (**57**).

Edward initially commissioned his goldsmith, Adam, to cast a bronze chair to house the Stone. Adam's bill claiming payment of expenses indicates that some parts had been completed when work was abandoned on 1 August 1297, probably because Edward needed the money to finance his campaign in Flanders. The design, which has close parallels with metalwork and masonry at Canterbury Cathedral, was retained. But Edward ordered Walter of Durham, his painter, to build a wooden chair instead (**colour plate 11**). This was completed by 1300–01, when Walter was paid 100

57 *The tomb of Edward I in Westminster Abbey, with St Edward's Shrine visible in the background. The (later) inscription on the tomb reads* Edwardus Primus Scottorum Malleus: *Edward the First, Hammer of the Scots.* The Dean and Chapter of Westminster Abbey

shillings. Walter also decorated and gilded the chair and attached two small leopards, carved, painted and gilded at a cost of 13s 4d. This decoration is presumably the patterns of birds in foliage and animals on a gilt ground, with the portrait on the Chair's backrest of either Edward the Confessor or Edward I himself, his feet resting on a lion. Only faint traces of this now survive. The four gilt lions currently supporting the Chair date only from 1727, but replace originals which were added *c*.1509. According to the Wardrobe Accounts for 1299–1300, Walter was also paid £1 19s 7d 'for making a step at the foot of the new throne (*cathedra*), in which the Scottish stone is placed near the altar, before the shrine of St Edward'. The chair is officially known as St Edward's Chair but is widely referred to as the Coronation Chair from its subsequent function.

The Chair celebrated Edward's triumph over the Scots. It was both trophy case and reliquary, holding the Stone which had been sanctified by its presentation to St Edward. The Chair appears to have been intended specifically for use in St Edward's Chapel. Edward directed the Stone 'to be made the chair of the priest celebrant', whose duty it was to celebrate mass at St Edward's shrine, according to Rishanger. Harding's *Metrical Chronicle* (*c*.1470) celebrated the Stone's capture and installation in Westminster:

And as he [Edward I] came homewarde by Skone away,
The Regal there of Scotland then he brought,
And sent it forth, to Westmynster for ay
To be there in a Cheire clenely wrought

For a masse priest to syt in, when he ought:
Whiche there was standyng, besyde the shryne
In a Cheire of olde time made full fyne.

The Stone and Chair conveyed a powerful symbolism. Once used for the inauguration of Scottish kings, the Stone now sat priests in what was almost a shrine to Edward's subjugation of the Scots. Camden's *Reges, Reginae, Nobiles* (1600) records a Latin inscription on a plaque hung beside the Chair which, although its date is unclear, reinforced this symbolism:

> If either the Chronicles or silver-haired Faithfulness has anything of the truth, then, see, there is enclosed within this chair the celebrated stone which the excellent Jacob, the one-time Patriarch, placed at his head when he beheld the marvellous divinities of Heaven; that which Edward I bore from the Scots, plundering like a conqueror of renown, or like Mars, powerful in arms; vanquisher of the Scots, our own most mighty Hector, the ornament of the English, and the glory of the soldiery.

The Chair may also have been intended to raise the status of Westminster Abbey to that of a cathedral by giving it the throne or *cathedra* required. Reflecting its importance, the Chair would originally have been visible down the entire length of the abbey (**58**).

Despite its later history, there is no evidence that the Chair was originally intended for royal coronations. Although an inventory of 1307 refers to the chair in which the English and Scottish kings are crowned, this is of doubtful reliability. No English king had been crowned since the Chair was built and the passage concerned has been ruled through. Nevertheless, the Stone's political symbolism, derived from its use in the inauguration of Scottish kings and its capture by Edward, soon ensured its central role in English rituals of royalty.

THE CORONATION STONE

The origins of the coronation rite are obscure, but the practice became fashionable in western Europe after the Emperor Charlemagne was crowned by Pope Leo III in 800. Anglo-Saxon kings adopted the rites of coronation and anointment and were crowned at various locations, including Kingston-on-Thames and Winchester. But the first coronation in Westminster Abbey was that of William I ('the Conqueror') on 25 December 1066. Emphasising the occasion's political significance, William was crowned beside the tomb of Edward the Confessor (1042–66), the penultimate king of Anglo-Saxon England. William's coronation established a practice which survives to this day and has become inalienably linked with Westminster Abbey. Westminster Abbey holds the distinction of being a 'royal peculiar'. It is under the jurisdiction of the Crown and not the bishop whose diocese it is in, an exemption granted by the pope before the Reformation and never rescinded. Although the archbishop of Canterbury has officiated at most coronations, he does so as a result of the privilege originally conferred by William, and not through right, as he exercises no authority over the abbey.

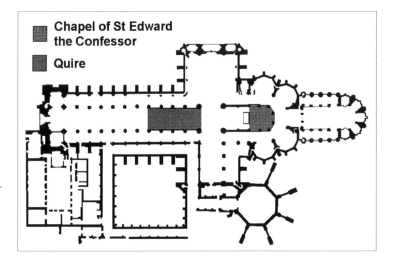

Chapel of St Edward the Confessor

Quire

58 Plan of Westminster Abbey, showing the location of St Edward's Chapel and the Coronation Chair

When stripped of later elements, such as coronation and anointment, the English and Scottish medieval king-making ceremonies both possess a combination of similar secular and ecclesiastical elements. Although royal succession was usually determined by inheritance in medieval England, the coronation ritual fossilises elements of an earlier mechanism for selecting kings. Medieval English monarchs were firstly 'elected' in Westminster Hall and lifted on to a marble seat known as the King's Bench. The coronation ceremony in Westminster Abbey was essentially the presentation of the monarch to his subjects, at which he pledged to preserve his people's rights. The king may then have returned to the King's Bench for the coronation feast. The election and feast were secular in nature. But the 'contract' between monarch and subjects was – and still is – witnessed and consecrated by the Church, which ritually invested the ruler with his kingship, each item of regalia symbolising an aspect of his new office. The Stone and Chair do not belong to the regalia but are incorporated in the coronation ceremony through tradition.

Every English monarch is traditionally believed to have been crowned on the Stone since its installation in St Edward's Chair. But the first English king whose coronation on the Stone is explicitly recorded is Henry IV (1399–1413), who was 'seated in the royal seat upon the stone which is called the regal stone of the kingdom of Scotland', according to the *Annals of Henry IV*. Henry Bolingbroke, Duke of Lancaster, became the first king of the House of Lancaster by deposing Richard II. To secure his newly-won kingship, Henry sought the legitimacy offered by an ostentatious coronation ceremony incorporating new elements (**colour plate 23**), including anointment with the holy oil of St Thomas, a rite previously denied to English kings by the pope. Dr Paul Binski has claimed that the Stone and Chair were first used in the English coronation ceremony as part of this legitimising process. But Henry might have been expected to emphasise the traditional nature of the ritual. Indeed, it is described as the ceremony 'in use up to the present time', details of which could be found in the records of Westminster Abbey and the archbishop of Canterbury. Henry's enthronement on the Stone and Chair is simply the earliest record of a traditional practice.

Two coronation portraits confirm this. One shows Richard II (1377–99) in majesty in the Coronation Chair (**colour plate 24**). Differences between the chair portrayed and the real Coronation Chair are attributable to artistic licence; for example, the acute gable on the backrest is omitted to avoid obscuring the lines of the king's portrait and crown. This proves that Richard was crowned in the Chair and, therefore, on the Stone. Although Richard's coronation is recorded in detail in Thomas Walsingham's *Historia Anglicana*, there is no reference to the Chair or Stone, possibly because these were already established and therefore unremarkable features of the ceremony.

But the coronation portrait of Edward II (**colour plate 25**) proves that English kings were crowned in the Chair and on the Stone from 1308, the first opportunity for its use in a coronation since it was installed in Westminster Abbey by Edward I. Edward II may have been crowned in the Chair out of respect for his father's memory and in tribute to his father's victory over the Scots. The portrait shows the Chair in what must have been close to its original form, with several features, including the pinnacles, which have not survived. The debate concerning the Stone's possible return to the Scots in the 1320s does not preclude its use in Edward's coronation. Although Edward claimed to be prepared to relinquish the Stone in 1324, he did not actually do so. And despite a writ authorising the Stone's return in 1328, it remained at Westminster.

Since 1308, the Stone, housed beneath the seat of the Coronation Chair, has played a central role in the making of almost every English and British monarch. In 700 years, only five monarchs have not been crowned on the Stone. Edward V died in 1483 before his coronation, which had already been prepared, could be held. Lady Jane Grey was proclaimed but not crowned during her nine-day reign in 1553. Mary (1553–58) preferred to be crowned in a chair that had been blessed by the pope because her Protestant half-brother, Edward VI (1547–53), had been crowned in the Chair. William and Mary's joint coronation in 1689 posed a unique problem which was partially solved by making a second chair, now in the Westminster Abbey museum, for Mary. The Stone, however, was not copied. And finally, Edward VIII abdicated in 1936 before his coronation. From Edward II, 28 English and subsequently British monarchs have been crowned on the Stone. Queen Victoria (1837–1901) was crowned on the Stone twice, as Queen in 1837 and as Empress of India in 1876, and also occupied the Chair at her Golden Jubilee celebration in 1887.

Although many of these coronations were notable occasions, the Stone played an unobtrusive, though central, role. Indeed, the Stone appears to have remained invisible, hidden not only beneath the seat of the Coronation Chair but also behind the monarch's ceremonial garments; Queen Victoria described how, at her Golden Jubilee, 'my robes were beautifully draped on the chair'. The Chair was also decked in rich cloths. Royal accounts for Richard III's coronation in 1483 list 'baudekin, to cover St Edward's Chair', while Elizabeth's coronation accounts of 1558 list 'Cloth of silver incarnate [i.e. shot with crimson], for covering St Edward's Chair, 18 yards. Fringe of red silk and silver, 7lbs and 3oz'. And for Charles II's coronation in 1660, the Chair was 'covered all over with cloth of gold', according to Ogilby's account. This was the pattern until Queen Victoria's Golden Jubilee in 1887, when the Chair was varnished brown and velvet armrests were added. The Chair still bears the accumulated scars where these cloths were secured.

Some ceremonies stand out as exceptional. In 1657, Oliver Cromwell was installed as Lord Protector in Westminster Hall by being seated 'in the Chair of Scotland', 'set under a prince-like canopy of state', according to Prestwick's account. The Chair and Stone were moved from Westminster Abbey especially for the ceremony, the only occasion on which the Stone left the Abbey between 1297 and 1950. The ceremony reflects Cromwell's position as king in all but name, as well as emphasising the importance attached to the Stone.

Only rarely have dissenting opinions about the Stone's role been expressed and then only by those not directly involved in the proceedings. Warner argued in *The History of Ireland* (1763) that 'the coronation of the Kings of England over this stone seems to confirm its title of the Stone of destiny; but it reflects no great honour on the learning or understanding of the nation, to retain a remnant of such ridiculous Pagan superstition in so important and solemn an act'. But rather than a source of criticism or embarrassment, others have celebrated the Stone's past. To Dean Stanley, the Stone, although 'embedded in the heart of the English monarchy', was:

> an element of poetic, patriarchal, heathen times, which ... carries back our thoughts to races and customs now almost extinct; a link which unites the Throne of England to the traditions of Tara and Iona, and connects the charm of our complex civilisation with the forces of our mother earth, the stocks and stones of savage nature.

Their close association with the monarchy has made the Stone and Chair the target of occasional protests and attacks. In 1914, Suffragettes hung a dorothy bag containing a blast bomb, comprising two bicycle bells packed with explosives and surrounded by nuts and bolts, from one of the pinnacles on the back of the Chair. Both the Chair and, to a lesser extent, the Stone sustained more damage in this explosion than they did during two world wars. In 1915, both Stone and Chair were moved to the Chapter House crypt to protect them from air raids. More elaborate measures were taken during the Second World War: while the Chair was sent for safekeeping in Gloucester Cathedral, the Stone was buried secretly in the Islip Chapel and the governor of Canada entrusted with its location in case Britain should fall. Apart from coronations and Cromwell's installation, these are the only occasions on which both the Stone and Chair have been moved from St Edward's Chapel.

In contrast to medieval practices, modern coronation ceremonies do not immediately follow the death of the preceding monarch. There is no longer a requirement to avoid an interregnum at all costs. For example, King George VI died on 6 February 1952; Princess Elizabeth 'ascended the throne' the same day and was proclaimed queen on 8 February. But because of the planning required for such a grand state occasion, her coronation did not take place until 2 June 1953, the first major royal event to be televised.

Elizabeth's coronation was the last occasion on which the Stone performed its historic function. Then, as in previous coronations, the Chair and Stone were moved from St Edward's Chapel and placed centrally in the Quire, in front of the high altar (**59**). In the Chair and on the Stone, the Queen made her oath, was presented with the Bible and anointed. She was then vested in the royal robes and the regalia taken one by one from the high altar. Firstly, the Golden Spurs were presented to the Queen, then four swords from the regalia were presented to their bearers standing on either side of the Chair. The

59 *Westminster Abbey as a ceremonial stage, laid out for the coronation of Queen Elizabeth II in 1953. The Coronation Chair, holding the Stone of Destiny, forms the focus of the ceremony. The Throne Chair, on the steps behind the Coronation Chair, is occupied after the coronation is completed*

Sword of the Offering was then handed to the Queen herself before being passed to the Dean of Westminster. Next were the royal armills or bracelets. The Queen then rose from the Chair to be invested with the Stole Royal and Robe Royal Cloth of Gold, before receiving the Orb, the Coronation Ring and the Sceptre with the Cross and the Rod with the Dove. This part of the ceremony culminated with the archbishop of Canterbury then raising the crown aloft and placing it on the Queen's head.

After her coronation, the Queen rose from the Coronation Chair and moved to the Throne Chair on the steps behind it. The steps represent a survival of the *pulpitum* on which medieval coronations were conducted (**colour plate 23**). These features perform similar functions to the Moot Hill at Scone. They raise the monarch above his or her subjects, allowing those assembled to witness the spectacle of the coronation ceremony, but also emphasise the monarch's elevated status and the social distance between the monarch and even those privileged enough to attend the coronation.

Although the ceremony has clearly changed over the centuries, many of its key elements retain a similar form and unaltered symbolism to those found in the medieval coronation rite. The ceremony by which Elizabeth was crowned is directly descended from the medieval coronation rite: English kings were crowned on the Stone from 1308, the coronation rite was first celebrated in Westminster Abbey in

1066, while the Stone's role in the making of kings is recorded as early as 1249, but probably originated much earlier. Although housed in Edinburgh Castle since 1996, the royal warrant authorising the restoration of the Stone to Scotland stipulates that the Commissioners of the Regalia of Scotland are responsible for making appropriate arrangements to ensure that all future coronations should take place upon the Stone at Westminster. Despite its return to Scotland, the Stone still retains its historic and symbolic role and its long association with Westminster Abbey.

ENGLISH MYTHS

English myths about the Stone of Destiny first appeared soon after its installation in Westminster Abbey, stimulated by the Stone's capture and arrival in London, the political symbolism invested in it and its increased accessibility to a new and wider audience. The earliest surviving English mythological reference to the Stone, *La Piere d'Escoce* (*c*.1307), draws on a Scottish version of the Stone's mythical origins. But a distinctively English origin myth for the Stone soon emerged. This approached the Stone from a different perspective and with a contrasting objective, focusing not on the peoples who brought the Stone to Scotland but on the origins and Biblical associations of the Stone itself. Reflecting the Stone's capture and installation in Westminster Abbey, English myths attest the Stone's reinvention as both a symbol of the Scots' conquest and a sacred relic.

The dominant English version of the myth is first recorded in William Rishanger's *Chronica et Annales* (*c*.1327). Rishanger refers to 'the regal stone, which Jacob placed under his head when he went from Bersabee to Haran'. This may have been prompted by Scottish myths of the Stone's eastern Mediterranean origin, but it does not belong to the Scottish tradition. Instead, Rishanger was inspired by the Book of Genesis (28:10-13, 18, 22):

> Jacob left Beersheba and set out for Haran. When he had reached a certain place he passed the night there, since the sun had set. Taking one of the stones to be found at that place, he made it his pillow and lay down where he was. He had a dream: a ladder was there, standing on the ground with its top reaching to heaven; and there were angels of God going up it and coming down. And God was there, standing over him, saying, 'I am God ... I will give to you and your descendants the land on which you are lying ...'. Then Jacob awoke from his sleep and said, 'Truly, God is in this place and I never knew it!'. He was afraid and said, 'How awe-inspiring this place is! This is nothing less than a house of God; this is the gate of heaven!'. Rising early in the morning, Jacob took the stone he had used for his pillow, and set it up as a monument ... 'This stone I have set up as a monument shall be a house of God'.

Jacob's Dream embodies the concept of the *axis mundi* and this powerful imagery inspired several medieval works of art (**colour plate 26**).

The origins of the tradition identifying the Stone with Jacob's Pillow are unclear.

Rishanger's familiarity with this passage may have led him to equate them, possibly reflecting his ignorance of Scottish versions of the Stone's mythical origins. More probably, Rishanger was drawing on an existing, politically-motivated myth and this is supported by the prophecy's appearance in the earlier *La Piere d'Escoce*. The Jacob tradition, which also featured in the inscription recorded by Camden, may have originated within the abbey itself. Its function was to identify the Stone as an important holy relic and to invest it with a symbolic significance which differed from that expressed by its prophecy. Instead, the implication was that, just as God gave territory to Jacob, He too had given Scotland to Edward I and his successors.

The Stone was popularly known as Jacob's Stone throughout its stay in Westminster Abbey, and the tradition of Jacob's Pillow remains prominent in the Stone's mythology. An engraving of the catafalque of Anne of Denmark, Queen of James I of England and VI of Scotland, who died in 1619, refers explicitly to this myth. Anne is depicted lying on her tomb with her head resting on 'Jacob's Stone' while, above her, the queen's soul is shown ascending a ladder to heaven (**60**).

This emphasis on the Stone's Biblical origins is not confined to medieval myths. Increased interest in the Stone during the mid-nineteenth century attracted religious interpretations of its origins and significance. John Barnett identified it as the holy stone kept in the first temple at Jerusalem, venerated by David as 'the stone which the builders rejected' and honoured as the 'foundation pillar' on which Joshua made the Israelites swear their allegiance to God. Marrying the Old Testament with the Stone's mythology, Barnett claimed that the Stone was taken by the prophet Jeremiah and the remnants of the tribe of Judah after the temple's destruction by the Babylonians. The Stone then accompanied the children of Israel on their delivery from Egypt, in the wilderness and from there to Ireland.

The Stone's Biblical origin was a popular theme in England between the 1880s and 1939, periodically stimulated by renewed interest in the Stone and its mythology on the coronations of Edward VII (1902), George V (1911) and George VI (1937). The Association of British Israelites eagerly claimed the Stone as evidence that the Britons were descended from the Israelites. Mrs G.A. Rogers' *The Coronation Chair and England's Interest In It* (1881) was the most popular of several publications to advance this theory, its eighth edition appearing in 1924. Inspired by Rishanger's tradition, Rogers sought to prove that the Stone then in Westminster Abbey was the same stone on which Jacob laid his head, using scriptural references and parallels with sacred stones mentioned in the Bible.

Guided more by spiritual beliefs than analytical abilities, many of those advocating the Stone's Biblical origins claimed to have found evidence in its physical form. Barnett attributed the iron rings to the Israelites' 40 years in the wilderness:

> there are on the Stone remains of rings which a pole may have been thrust through so as to sling it for carriage on men's shoulders, in which way no doubt it was carried, together with the Ark [of the Covenant], through the wanderings of the people, until they took possession of the Land of Promise.

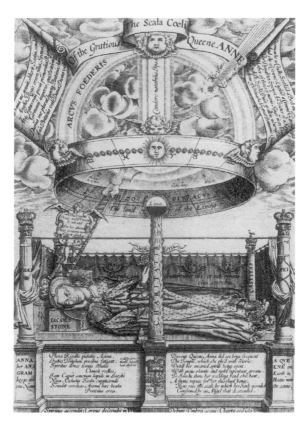

60 *An engraving of the catafalque of Anne of Denmark, Queen of James VI and I, in 1619. She is depicted lying on her tomb, with her head resting on Jacob's Stone while her spirit can be seen on the top rung of the ladder ascending to heaven.* RCIN 601440. The Royal Collection, Her Majesty the Queen

Referring to the Stone's flaw, the Rev J.H. Allen asked: 'Could it be possible that rent was made when and because Moses smote the rock when he was told to speak to it?'. Adam Rutherford was convinced: 'How came the great crack in this treasured stone? ... we have record in the Scriptures [Numbers 20:5-11] that it was struck by Moses in order to give the Israelites water to drink in the desert, thus accounting for the large fissure still to be seen in the side of the stone'. Such claims are easily dismissed, but they provide a revealing insight into the Stone's interpretation from a Biblical perspective.

British imperial attitudes were also influential in the perception of the Stone's significance. As early as 1868, the Stone was invested with a powerful symbolism and venerated as 'the one primeval monument which binds together the whole Empire', according to Dean Stanley. This sentiment dominated English perceptions of the Stone during the first half of the twentieth century. Rutherford proudly proclaimed the Stone to be 'the most precious emblem of the greatest empire the world has ever known' (**61**) and in 1924 even the Royal Commission on Historical Monuments (England) described the Stone as 'that strange palladium of the Empire'.

Two world wars also influenced interpretations of the Stone. During the First World War, Lt Col. Spencer Acklom described it as 'the stone pillar of our national identification'; and during the Second World War, F.T. Perry believed the Stone was 'the magnet of the empire that binds all the people in one', symbolising 'an ever-extending, world-wide kingdom – the

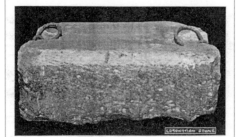

"This stone which I have set for pillar shall be God's House"
GENESIS 28, 22

By kind permission of the Dean and Chapter of Westminster

The Coronation Stone

THE MOST PRECIOUS EMBLEM
OF THE
GREATEST EMPIRE
THE WORLD HAS EVER KNOWN

"Thine house and thy kingdom shall be established for ever
before thee: thy throne shall be established for ever."
II SAMUEL 7, 16

61 *The Stone of Destiny as a symbol of imperial power. An illustration from Adam Rutherford's* The Coronation Chair and the Stone of Destiny (1937)

foundation-stone of an empire'. Despite Britain's post-war decline as an imperial power, the same theme is expressed in the subtitle of F.W. Connon's *The Stone of Destiny, or the Stone that Binds a Commonwealth* (1951).

The Stone and its prophecy were used to justify British imperialism. In 1910, Watson saw the Stone as 'an essential feature in the coronation ceremony of the monarchs of the greatest Empire on which the sun has shone. Truly the ancient ... prophecy of the all- dominion of them who sit upon this stone has been more than accomplished!'. The Stone's perceived origin among the Israelites was believed to confer a religious sanction upon the British Empire and its rulers. Rutherford claimed that 'The present place of the Stone of Israel, in the Coronation Chair of the greatest empire the world has ever known, beautifully symbolises Christ in His office of King of Kings and Lord of Lords, for ... "all nations shall serve and obey Him"'.

Acklom claimed that Old Testament accounts of royal inauguration rituals 'bear a striking similarity to the coronation of our British kings ... particularly ... King George Vth. The terms of our beautiful [coronation] service appear so purely Scriptural and Israelitish'. Identifying the Stone as 'the Pillar of Witness and the Throne of David', E.M. Shaw even claimed that 'King George V is descended from David'. Similarly, Rutherford concluded that 'the British Coronation Stone ... is none other than the Stone of Israel. Its possession by the British race ... is a token (1) that the British nation is the House of Joseph, (2) that the Royal House of Britain is the Royal House of David'.

124

These views reflect wider developments, particularly George V's role in reinventing the British monarchy as a symbol of national unity, including the annual Christmas Day broadcasts to the nation, begun in 1932, and his Silver Jubilee celebrations in 1935. But they were still being expressed during the 1950s. The Stone's removal from Westminster Abbey prompted *Brith*, the magazine of the Society for Proclaiming Britain is Israel, to assert that:

> The Stone is still and ever will be the 'Throne of the Lord'. It does not belong to any nation or land. It belongs to God and is entrusted by Him to the Royal House and Seed of David and is in their possession by right, as the will of God.

The British Israelites were not the only group to invest a Biblical significance in the Stone. Freemasons claimed a wider range of Biblical symbolism for it. According to A.E. Waite's *A New Encyclopaedia of Freemasonry* (1921), the Stone was not only Jacob's pillow, but also the stone from which the angel guided Adam and Eve to Paradise, the top of the altar raised by Abraham for the sacrifice of his son Isaac, the capstone of the First Temple at Jerusalem, and a sacred object treasured by the Jews after the temple's destruction.

Against this background it scarcely seems surprising that magical powers were still being attributed to the Stone into the 1950s. According to Perry, it was prophesied that 'whosoever stumbleth against that stone it shall grind them to powder, or scatter them as the chaff of the summer threshing floor'. But as Perry's book was published in 1940, when German invasion was imminent, his comments may understandably represent wishful thinking. And, as late as 1951, *Brith* warned about the 'Synagogue of Satan': 'The stone would be invaluable to them. Should it fall into their possession much harm will be wrought to the whole world'.

THE STONE IN ENGLISH LITERATURE

Quite apart from the extensive body of English mythology that developed around the Stone of Destiny during its 700-year stay in Westminster Abbey, references to the Stone appear widely in English literature since the sixteenth century. In conjunction with the myths, these literary appearances give an impression of the range of meaning invested in the Stone. Not only did perceptions of the Stone change over time, but it is clear that contrasting views about the Stone were also held. While those interested in its history, mythology and royal associations were awestruck, others were singularly unimpressed with its appearance. In contrast, 'H.R. (née F)' claimed in 1854 that the Stone had changed for the better:

> Thirty years ago, the Coronation Stone ... stood under a very old chair, and was a bluish irregular block of stone, similar both in colour and shape to stepping-stones in the shallow rivers of the north of England. It is *now* a very nice hewn block, nicely fitted into the frame under the seat of a renovated chair. It does not look at all like the old stone of former days.

The Stone's literary appearances were guaranteed partly by its historical and symbolic significance but also by the fact that it was housed in one of the most popular tourist attractions in Britain. In 1868, Dean Stanley described the Stone as 'probably the chief object of attraction to the innumberable visitors of the Abbey'. Indeed, Stanley cited the unwanted attention received by the Chair as evidence of this: 'the very disfigurements of the Chair, scratched over from top to bottom with the names of inquisitive visitors, proves not only the reckless irreverence of the intruders, but also the universal attraction of the relic'. The Stone maintained this status for many decades. In 1924, the Royal Commission still claimed that, 'Whatever was its original form, and whatever the origin of the sacredness attached to it ... this Stone is surely the most venerable and mysterious object now to be seen in the Abbey'. The Stone was an object of perennial fascination, every aspect of it attracting attention and drawing comment.

References to the Stone did not become common in English literature until the Elizabethan period, when the rise of antiquarianism stimulated interest. The *Historie of Scotland* in Holinshed's *Chronicles* (1577) was based on Bellenden's translation of Boece's *History*. This gave English readers access to Scottish traditions concerning the Stone, including its prophecy, for the first time. William Camden's *Britannia* (1586) also contained a brief account of Scottish traditions concerning the Stone and a version of the prophecy. The Stone also caught Shakespeare's attention, but appears not to have impressed him; he described it memorably, if unflatteringly, as 'A base foul Stone, made precious by the foil / Of England's Chair' in *Richard III* (Act 5, Scene 3; probably produced in 1594, printed in 1597).

The Stone also attracted foreign visitors during this period. It was seen by L. von Widel in 1584–85, Frederick, Duke of Württemberg, in 1592 and by Justus Zinzerling (Jodocus Sincerus), a Thuringian-born doctor of law at Basle, *c*.1610. In their accounts of their visits, von Widel and Frederick repeated the myth of the Stone as Jacob's Pillow, although Zinzerling mistakenly referred to it as Abraham's pillow.

The accession of James VI of Scotland, as James I, to the English throne in 1603 produced a surge of interest in the Stone and its prophecy. The Scots believed that the ancient prophecy that they would reign wherever the Stone was placed was at last fulfilled by James' accession. Moreover, the prophecy and the Stone's presence in London were said to have reconciled many Scots to the Union.

The translation of Camden's *Britannia* into English by Philemon Holland (1610) and others during the seventeenth and eighteenth centuries stimulated additional interest by making the Stone's mythology and prophecy accessible to a wider readership:

> Except old fawes be vaine,
> And wits of wisards blind:
> The Scots in place must raigne:
> Where they this stone shall finde.

The Stone enjoyed a higher literary profile over the following decades, featuring in pseudo-historical works such as Michael Drayton's *Poly-Olbion* (1622):

Our Longshanks, Scotland's scourge, who to the Orcads raught
His sceptre, and with him from wild Albania brought
The reliques of her crown (by him first placed here)
The seat on which her kings inaugurated were.

John Selden's 'Illustrations', annotations to Drayton's *Poly-Olbion*, included a brief account of the Stone's mythical origins, but warned of 'The Scottish stories (on whose credit ... I importune you not to rely)'.

Writers of this period were attuned to the Stone's renewed symbolic and political significance. John Speed's *The History of Great Britaine* (1623) referred to Edward I's removal of 'the Marble Chaire, in which the Kings of Scotland were wont to be crowned', noting that:

This Chaire is the same upon which was engraven the famous Propheticall Distichon:
    If Fates goe right, where ere this stone is pight,
    The Regall race of Scots shall rule that place.
Which by whomsoever it was written, we who now live, finde it happily accomplished.

A similar account appears in John Weever's *Ancient Funerall Monuments within the United Monarchie of Great Britaine, Ireland, and the Islands Adjacent* (1631). This gives the first wide-ranging account of the Stone's history, mythology and literary appearances. These various sources attest a continuing fascination with the prophecy and its apparent fulfilment.

The Stone's remarkable mythology, history and function often led to it being described in superlatives. In 1719, John Toland described the Stone as 'the antientest respected monument in the world; for tho' some others may be more antient as to duration, yet thus superstitiously regarded they are not'. This was an enduring theme. In the twentieth century, S.F. Bowser labelled the Stone as 'The oldest relic in history', while to Rutherford it was 'the most important, the most wonderful, the most sublime stone in the world!'.

But attitudes concerning the Stone were changing, even in Toland's day. Despite the Stone's Biblical and royal associations, many commentators were unable to see beyond its odd and unprepossessing appearance and began to express criticism. Visiting London in 1710, Zacharius Conrad von Uffenbach noted the discrepancy between the Stone and George Buchanan's description of it:

We also noticed the two wooden coronation chairs in the Chapel of St Edward the Confessor. They are so wretched and smoke-blackened that I should not care to have them among my household gear. They are, nevertheless, remarkable for their antiquity, and especially for the use to which they have been put. Under the chair ... we saw the famous stone of the Patriarch Jacob. I was vastly amazed that it was not of *lapidem Marmoreum rudem*, as Buchanan ... describes it ... but, as was quite obvious, a great block of pure sandstone, which has nothing in common with marble either in texture or grain. I should much have liked to have scraped off a little with my knife, which would have done little harm to this highly prized stone, but I dared not, for one is liable to punishment for even sitting on one of these chairs.

Such sceptical perceptions were not confined to foreign visitors. Joseph Addison's 'Sir Roger at Westminster Abbey' appeared in the *Spectator* in 1712:

> We were then conveyed to the two coronation chairs, where my old friend, after having heard that the stone underneath the most ancient of them, which was brought from Scotland, was called Jacob's pillar, sat himself down in the chair; and, looking like the figure of an old Gothic king, asked our interpreter what authority they had to say that Jacob had ever been in Scotland? The fellow, instead of returning him an answer, told him that he hoped his honour would pay his forfeit. I could observe Sir Roger [de Coverley] a little ruffled up on being thus trepanned; but our guide not insisting upon his demand, the knight soon recovered his good humour, and whispered in my ear, that if Will Wimble were with us, and saw those two chairs, it would go hard but he would get a tobacco stopper out of one or t'other of them.

In *The Citizen of the World* (1762), Oliver Goldsmith expressed contempt for the fabrications told by the abbey guides and for their extortionate charges. Goldsmith's disdain extended to both the Stone and the Chair:

> 'Look ye there, gentlemen', says he, pointing to an old oak chair, 'there's a curiosity for ye; in that chair the kings of England were crowned, you see also a stone underneath, and that stone is Jacob's pillow'. I could see no curiosity either in the oak chair or the stone; could I, indeed, behold one of the old kings of England seated in this, or Jacob's head laid up on the other, there might be something curious in the sight; but in the present case, there was no more reason for my surprize than if I should pick a stone from their streets and call it a curiosity, merely because one of their kings happened to tread upon it as he passed.

And a Mr Hutton, visiting from the provinces in 1784, mused about the Stone that 'its being hard and cold might very well suit the brawny posteriors of a northern monarch'.

By 1781, these dismissive views, openly sceptical about the Stone's mythology and contemptuous of its unsophisticated appearance, produced a climate of opinion in which the very authenticity of the Stone could be challenged openly. The long debate had begun.

7

THE STONE RETURNS

It is still believed that the Stone was peculiarly connected with the fortunes of the Scottish race.   W.F. Skene, *The Coronation Stone* (1869)

Reflecting its symbolic importance, efforts to return the Stone of Destiny to Scotland began as early as the 1320s, but without success. More recently, the Stone has been removed from Westminster Abbey on two occasions. The first, in 1950–51, was unauthorised, clandestine and ultimately unsuccessful, although it grabbed both headlines and the public imagination. The second, in 1996, was in complete contrast. Announced by the prime minister and authorised by a royal warrant, the Stone was returned to its ancient homeland amid much pomp and ceremony. This concluding chapter looks at the contentious issue and eventful history of the Stone's rightful ownership and location and at the various attempts, successful and unsuccessful, legal and illegal, to restore the Stone to Scotland.

EARLY ATTEMPTS

It has often been asserted that the Scots never sought the Stone of Destiny's return after its seizure by Edward I in 1296. In Scotland, this is frequently claimed as evidence that Edward did not take the real Stone but was fooled into taking a substitute instead. But this does not stand up to scrutiny. The Scots began the long quest to regain the Stone on which their kings were inaugurated within a generation of its removal from Scone.

Admittedly, the *Instructiones* and Bisset's *Processus* made no attempt to reclaim the Stone in 1301. The *Processus* did draw the pope's attention to 'the royal seat which this king of England forcibly took away with him'. Bisset may have hoped that if the pope found in the Scots' favour, he would advise that the Stone be returned to Scotland. But Bisset's plea to the pope concerned Scotland's very existence as an independent nation; the Stone's possession was, by comparison, a minor consideration. Moreover, the accession of Robert I in 1306 and the long Scottish War of Independence that followed ruled out any prospect of the Stone's imminent return.

The Scots were in a stronger position by the 1320s, following their victory at Bannockburn in 1314 and a series of raids into northern England over the following decade. Having reasserted Scotland's *de facto* independence, Robert sought to secure this with a negotiated peace treaty in which Edward II renounced English claims to Scotland. At peace negotiations held at York during the winter of 1324, the Scots presented their conditions. The *Life of Edward II* records that:

The Scots also demanded that the royal stone should be restored to them, which Edward I had long ago taken from Scotland and placed at Westminster by the tomb of St Edward. This stone was of famous memory amongst the Scots, because upon it the kings of Scotland used to receive the symbols of authority and the sceptre.

Although acknowledging the Stone's symbolic significance, Edward II dismissed it as unimportant within the overall context of the negotiations:

> we know that my father, when Scotland had been conquered, took with him the famous royal stone as a sign of victory; and if we were to restore it we should seem basely to repudiate the right thus acquired. Nevertheless, we should make little difficulty about returning the stone, if their other demands were not beyond all reason ... But as their demands are too damaging to us, they shall return home unsatisfied.

Edward II's refusal to recognise Robert as the independent king of an independent Scotland ensured that the talks were inconclusive. The Stone remained at Westminster.

In 1327, the Scots renewed the struggle for recognition of their independence on two fronts, taking the war to the English in both Northumbria and Ulster. In October, Robert dictated his peace terms and the English deliberated over his demands throughout the winter. The English parliament eventually met at York to approve the concessions required and, on 1 March 1328, Edward III renounced the claims of English rule, dominion or superiority over Scotland, admitting that he and his predecessors had afflicted both England and Scotland in pursuing those claims, and recognising Robert as King of Scots. An English envoy then travelled to Edinburgh to finalise the terms of the peace treaty with Robert and the Scottish parliament. The treaty was concluded on 17 March and ratified by the English parliament at Northampton on 4 May.

The Treaty of Edinburgh-Northampton enshrined Scotland's right to be 'separate in all things from the kingdom of England, entire, free, and quit, and without any subjection, servitude, claim or demand'. And, following an English petition, the pope lifted his excommunication of the Scottish king, imposed for killing Sir John ('the Red') Comyn in 1306. With the sole exception of anointment, Robert, already bed-ridden and with less than a year to live, had achieved his goals at last.

Contrary to modern popular opinion, there was no provision for the Stone's return to Scotland in the Treaty of Edinburgh-Northampton. The treaty also ignored the claims of the disinherited, those nobles who were deprived of their estates during the War of Independence. Both issues were soon linked. On 1 July 1328, a writ issued under the privy seal of Edward III informed the abbot and monks of Westminster that:

> his Council had, in his Parliament held at Northampton, agreed that the Stone upon which the Kings of Scotland are [sic] accustomed to be placed at their coronation should be sent to Scotland, and requiring the Abbot and monks, in whose custody it was, to deliver it to the sheriffs of London, who were to cause it to be carried to the Queen Mother.

Edward II had been deposed by his wife, Isabella, and her lover, Roger de Mortimer, in 1327 and was later murdered. And although Edward III was crowned in 1327, he was only fourteen years old; the real power behind the throne was his mother. A second writ ordered the sheriffs to receive the Stone from the abbot and deliver it to Isabella in northern England or Berwick-upon-Tweed, where she intended to negotiate compensation with the Scots for the English disinherited. Isabella evidently planned to use the Stone as a bargaining chip with the Scots, but her plan was thwarted. The sheriffs reported that the Stone's surrender was blocked by the people of London.

The Stone may have acquired such a strong symbolism in the thirty years since its installation in Westminster Abbey that Londoners could not relinquish it. Despite the realities of the Treaty of Edinburgh-Northampton, the Stone was a very tangible symbol of English triumph, something concrete to show for the long and costly war against the Scots. Indeed, the Stone's retention may reflect Londoners' reaction to what some in England referred to as the 'Shameful Peace'. But it would be naïve to interpret this event simply as an expression of the common will. Indeed, the *Chronicle of Geoffrey le Baker of Swinbrook* records that the abbot of Westminster helped to frustrate plans to return the Stone to Scotland. This suggests that the abbot, perhaps motivated by the Stone's perceived status as a holy relic, may have encouraged or even incited the protests. This episode reflects the political instability of the time, with the abbot of Westminster and/or sheriffs of London exploiting the monarchy's weakness and troublesome Londoners merely providing a convenient excuse for not returning the Stone.

Scotland had assured its status as an independent sovereign nation, but the Stone stayed at Westminster. In contrast, the Black Rood, the Scots' fragment of the True Cross, was returned to Scotland, only to be lost to the English again at the Battle of Neville's Cross, near Durham, in 1346. Subsequently kept in Durham Cathedral, the Black Rood was destroyed during the Reformation.

The Scottish king was also captured at Neville's Cross. Under the Treaty of Berwick of 1357, David II (1329–71) was only released on condition that the Scots paid 10,000 merks a year for ten years, a crippling sum for a poor country ravaged by warfare. After the Scots defaulted, Edward III proposed that the ransom could be waived providing that if David died childless he would accept either the English king or an English prince as the next king of Scots. But the kingdoms were not to be united and the 'King of England and Scotland' was to be crowned twice, in separate ceremonies at Westminster and Scone. As an added incentive, the Stone would be returned to Scotland. The eleventh article of the agreement between Edward and David was that 'The King, after having been crowned King of England, to come regularly to the kingdom of Scotland, and to be crowned King at Scone, in the royal chair, which is to be delivered up by the English'. David, influenced by his long years at the English court, accepted. Although the Scottish chroniclers claimed that the proposal was summarily dismissed by the parliament that sat at Scone in March 1364, it was debated before being rejected. It is unclear if any significance was attached to the offer to return the Stone. Again, more important issues were at stake.

These were the only recorded occasions on which the Stone's repatriation was raised during the Middle Ages. As the Stone's symbolic significance to the Scottish kingship diminished with its continued absence and as Scone declined as a royal centre, its return became less important. With the coronation of Scottish kings at other royal centres, the historic and symbolic links between the inauguration ceremony, Scone and the Stone disappeared. And with the accession of James VI of Scotland to the English throne in 1603, the Stone's rightful ownership and location ceased to be contentious.

THE DEBATE REOPENED: 1884–1950

The Stone of Destiny's ownership and location remained uncontested until the late nineteenth century. Increased interest in the Stone's history and mythology during the mid-nineteenth century was not accompanied by calls for the Stone's repatriation to Scotland. The Stone's continued presence at Westminster was not an issue as long as Scots believed that they benefited from the union with England and while both nations prospered as the British Empire approached its zenith.

Ireland, however, was very different. Ireland joined the United Kingdom in 1801 but the issues of land reform and Catholic emancipation, the famine of 1845–50 and the growing struggle for independence produced great tensions. The 1880s was an eventful decade in Irish politics, the 'land war' of 1879–82 ultimately leading to Gladstone's unsuccessful Home Rule Bill of 1886. There was increased interest in the traditions concerning the Stone's Irish origins or associations during this period. In 1884, C.S. Kenney, MP for Barnsley, complained in the House of Commons that the public notice attached to the Coronation Chair had been altered and now omitted all reference to the coronation of Irish kings on the Stone. With growing awareness of the Stone's mythical Irish origins, the presence in Westminster Abbey of what was widely believed to be the *Lia Fáil* assumed a political significance during the 1880s. The Stone was invested with a new symbolism.

In 1884, some members of Clan na Gael, part of the Fenian movement seeking Irish independence through armed rebellion, plotted to seize the Stone. 'Henri Le Caron', the British intelligence officer Thomas Miller Beach, recounted the episode with evident incredulity in *Twenty-Five Years in the Secret Service: the Recollections of a Spy* (1892):

> Of all the schemes indulged in by the dynamite men, none seems to have been more far-fetched than that of the theft of a certain stone from within the walls of Westminster Abbey. This was the famous 'Stone of Scone', which serves as the seat of the Coronation-chair in the Abbey.
>
> To an outsider the possession of such a stone as this seems of no importance whatever. Yet, ludicrous as it may appear, the idea of securing it gave rise to a great enthusiasm and led to a very generous subscription with this object. According to the originators of the scheme, this 'Stone of Destiny' was really the property of Ireland for a thousand years before Christ, and upon it were crowned the Irish kings, for hundreds of years, on the sacred Hill of Tara. Its restoration to the land

of its original and only lawful owners, it was contended, would inspire confidence in the course then being pursued, and the people would be strengthened by the well-known tradition 'that so long as this stone remained in Ireland, so long would she remain a united nation', while its loss to the English would work wonders.

Elaborate preparations were made for carrying out the scheme. Men were sent from America to work in conjunction with certain Fenians in London, and it was decided that some of the conspirators should secrete themselves in the Abbey, and at night seize the police, remove the stone, and pass it out through a window to others who would be in waiting outside to take it to a place of safety. For months these men waited and waited, but the opportunity never came, for one of the group gave the whole thing away to the police, and the detectives who surrounded the sacred edifice made the seizure impossible. In the end the three principals had to leave the country for fear of arrest.

Both the Stone and its prophecy, adapted to suit the context, were appropriated by the Irish nationalist cause.

Although never executed, the Clan na Gael plot is significant as the first recorded attempt to remove the Stone from Westminster Abbey illicitly. It also established the Stone's ownership as a contemporary political issue. This prefaced a series of attempts, both real and fictional, successful and unsuccessful, to retrieve the Stone over the next century. On all subsequent occasions, however, the debate focused exclusively on the Stone's Scottish associations. Although the Stone and the *Lia Fáil* continued to be confused, the Irish dimension disappears.

The Scottish Home Rule Bill passed its second reading in the House of Commons by a substantial majority in 1913, but was dropped because of the First World War. And attempts to reintroduce it in 1924 and 1926 both failed. A nationalist movement emerged in its aftermath, leading in 1928 to the founding of the National Party of Scotland, which became the Scottish National Party (SNP) in 1934. It was within this political context that the modern debate concerning the Stone began.

David Kirkwood, Labour MP for Clydebank and Dumbarton Burghs, introduced a Private Members' Bill to the House of Commons in 1924 calling for the Stone to be restored to Scotland. Despite passing its first reading by 201 votes to 171, the bill failed to receive government support because of the limited parliamentary time available. But although the Stone remained at Westminster, Kirkwood's bill had successfully publicised the issue.

The failure of constitutional and legal moves almost inevitably inspired some Scottish patriots to seek alternative means of returning the Stone to Scotland. In 1929, Robert 'Bertie' Gray (**62**), a Glasgow monumental mason, made a replica of the Stone which he planned to substitute for the original. In a complex plan, not only would he have had to remove the real Stone from Westminster Abbey, but also take its replacement in. It is unclear if Gray intended to fool the abbey authorities into believing that they still had the genuine Stone or if it was simply an elaborate decoy to give Gray enough time to get the real Stone to Scotland before its loss was discovered. But the plot was leaked and the plan abandoned.

62 *The Stone snatchers, 1 (from left to right): Councillor Bertie Gray, Gavin Vernon, Ian Hamilton and Alan Stuart, 1951*

Other events focused attention on the Stone. Under pressure from Scottish historians, the surviving documents seized by Edward I in 1296 were returned to Scotland by the Public Record Office in London in the 1930s. This prompted Wendy Wood to parade along Edinburgh's Royal Mile waving a placard asking 'England Disgorges some of the Loot, but where is the Stone of Destiny?'. And in her autobiography, *Yours Sincerely for Scotland* (1970), Wood recollects how some Scots tried to seize the Kingston-on-Thames coronation stone. But this tit-for-tat attempt to deprive the English of their own stone was unsuccessful.

The Stone's contentious ownership also featured in contemporary Scottish fiction. Sir Compton Mackenzie's *The North Wind of Love* (1944) featured a plot to take the Stone from Westminster Abbey on St Andrew's Day 1932 and return it to Scotland:

> it fell to Mr South to make the journey down to London for the proposed rescue of the Stone of Destiny from Westminster ... to James Maxwell was accorded the honour and glory of superintending through Tom Fletcher the actual removal of the Stone from the Abbey, and the arrangements for the first car that was to bear it as far as the end of the Embankment. Here another car was to bear it to another rendezvous in the Midlands and so on in a zigzag until the Border was reached, where no less than twelve cars would bear it back and forth in Scotland.

The last car was to 'drive to the secret spot where the Stone was to be buried', but the plan was aborted after it was leaked. And in Nigel Tranter's *The Freebooters* (1950), a letter to the press 'urged an immediate removal of the Stone of Destiny' from the Abbey. Strangely prescient, this novel was published only months before the Stone was taken from the Abbey.

THE STONE RETRIEVED: 1950–51

The highlight of all the attempts to remove the Stone of Destiny from Westminster Abbey is undoubtedly that of 1950–51. Until 1996, this was the only occasion on which the Stone was actually returned to Scotland. Although well known, this episode is worth recounting not only for the sheer audacity with which the operation was conducted, but also because it has had such a profound influence on subsequent Scottish attitudes towards the Stone.

The period after the Second World War saw another increase in nationalist sentiment in Scotland. In 1945, Robert McIntyre won the Motherwell by-election to become the SNP's first member of parliament, only to lose his seat at the following general election. Frustration at the ballot box and concern at the centralising tendencies of the post-war Labour government led to the founding of the Scottish Convention by John MacCormick (**63**) in 1947. Launched in 1949, the National Covenant demanded home rule for Scotland within a federal system and within a year around one million Scots had signed (**64**). Against a rising tide of national consciousness and in desperation at the political *status quo*, the Stone was invested with a renewed significance. While the Palace of Westminster refused to relinquish any of its constitutional powers over Scotland, Westminster Abbey retained the Stone. The Stone symbolised the continued suppression of Scottish aspirations by an unsympathetic, even hostile, Establishment.

Ian Hamilton (**62–65**) had been aware of the Stone and its history from childhood. A 25-year-old law student at Glasgow University, where MacCormick was elected Lord Rector in 1950, Hamilton was a close associate of MacCormick's and was heavily involved with the Scottish Covenant. Hamilton resolved to restore the Stone to Scotland. In September 1950, he reconnoitred Westminster Abbey to assess whether the Stone could be extracted from the Coronation Chair and then removed from the Abbey. Having satisfied himself that it could, Hamilton recruited two fellow students, Alan Stuart (20) and Gavin Vernon (24), and Kay Matheson (21), a domestic science teacher (**64, 67**). Bertie Gray, by then a Glasgow city councillor and vice-chairman of the National Covenant, provided financial support.

The plan was bold but simple. The four waited until the Christmas holidays, when they would not be missed, and drove to London. Two Ford Anglias were used: one hired, the other belonging to Alan Stuart. The 400-mile (644km) journey, along wintry secondary roads, took 18 hours.

On Saturday 23 December, Hamilton hid himself in the abbey after closing time, intending to wait until the early hours before forcing a door near Poets' Corner to admit the others and remove the Stone. But Hamilton was discovered by a night-watchman. Unaware of the jemmy hidden under Hamilton's coat, the watchman assumed that Hamilton was homeless and offered him some money before ejecting him from the abbey. But this setback did not deter the group. The following night, Christmas Eve, another attempt was made. At four o'clock on Christmas morning they reversed one of the cars up a lane beside the abbey and into a builder's yard beside Henry VII's Chapel. While Matheson stayed in the car, the three men forced their way into the abbey through a door at Poets' Corner. From there they made for St Edward's Chapel, where they prized away

63 *John MacCormick (right), in the ceremonial gown of Rector of the University of Glasgow, and Ian Hamilton, 1951*

64 *The National Covenant, held by Ian Hamilton*

the wooden bevel securing the Stone in its recess beneath the seat of the Coronation Chair.

So far, so good. But the group was then plagued with a catalogue of errors, though balanced by good fortune in equal measure. On pulling the Stone out of the Chair, it crashed onto the stone floor and, by Hamilton's own admission, broke into two pieces. The natural flaw in the rock, detectable on earlier photographs, had given way, detaching a corner – about a quarter of its total mass – from the Stone. The fragments were placed

65 *Damaged photograph of the Stone snatchers, 2 (from left to right): Gavin Vernon, Kay Matheson and Ian Hamilton, 1951*

on an outstretched coat and dragged across the floor, down the Sanctuary steps, along the east aisle of the South Transept, and out through the Poets' Corner door; the Abbey authorities were able to trace the route the next morning from the tracks left on the floor. But the weight was considerable and, taking advantage of the mishap, Hamilton picked up the smaller piece and rushed it out to the waiting car where he placed it in the boot.

At that moment a policeman appeared out of the darkness. Hamilton and Matheson quickly feigned an embrace and, when questioned about their presence, claimed that they had arrived in London too late to find accommodation. The constable, taking pity on them, offered them cigarettes and, although a noise echoed from the abbey as Stuart and Vernon wrestled with the rest of the Stone, he failed to investigate. After a smoke and a chat, the policeman advised them to move on. The two drove off with the smaller fragment of the Stone, leaving their compatriots with the remainder.

Hamilton soon returned to the abbey, leaving Matheson with the car and the lesser part of the Stone. But there was no sign of Stuart, Vernon, or the bulk of the Stone. Emerging from the abbey, Hamilton stumbled across the broken Stone in the builder's yard outside. He then raced off to get the second car, which had been left in Millbank. Only when he got there did he realise that the keys were still in a pocket of the coat on which the Stone had been dragged from the abbey. Hamilton was forced to enter the abbey for the third time that night, this time searching on his hands and knees in the gloom for the keys, but to no avail.

Now desperate, Hamilton began to strike matches more in hope than expectation, as the area to be covered was extensive. He had all but given up when he stepped on the keys. Retrieving the second car, Hamilton retraced his way up the lane alongside the abbey for the fourth time that night. Fuelled with adrenalin, he managed to lift the Stone into the boot by himself and drove off. Luck was still with them. In the Old Kent Road, Hamilton chanced upon a dejected Stuart and Vernon, who had abandoned their mission when they

66 *Newspaper headlines announce the theft of the Stone of Destiny, 27 December 1950*

were unable to find the car keys. To avoid overloading the car, Vernon was left to make his own way home to Scotland.

Police issued a nationwide alert: 'Thieves with stolen Coronation Stone thought heading North by road'. Across northern England, off-duty policemen were hurriedly called from their Christmas lunches to man road blocks. All northbound traffic was stopped and searched in a huge operation to intercept the Stone before it reached Scotland. The Anglo-Scottish border was closed for the first time in centuries. But Hamilton and Stuart sped not north, but south. Successfully anticipating the police response, the pair drove around southern England, from Marlborough (Wiltshire) in the west to Rochester (Kent) in the east. Expecting to be arrested within hours, they dumped the Stone in an open field on Christmas morning. But as the day wore on their confidence increased and they returned to retrieve their prize. The Stone was then hidden in a wood near Rochester before the patriots headed north. Not until Doncaster, 150 miles (240km) north of London, were they stopped by police. But the pair talked themselves through and returned to a Scotland buzzing with news about the Stone's 'theft' (**66**).

The following week, Hamilton drove south again, on this occasion with another two companions, Bill Craig and Johnny Josselyn, and in a more powerful Armstrong Siddeley. But on returning to where they had concealed the Stone, they found a gypsy camp. After winning the gypsies' confidence, they retrieved the Stone. Substituting the Stone for the car's passenger seat, they concealed it beneath a travelling rug and, taking turns to sit on it, drove north. Travelling the back roads, they crossed the River Esk into Scotland between Longtown and Canonbie in the early hours of 31 December. The Stone was back in Scotland for the first time in 655 years.

On reaching Glasgow, Hamilton and the others were directed by Gray to the works of John Rollo, an executive committee member of the National Covenant, at Bonnybridge. There, on New Year's Day 1951, Rollo built a crate for the Stone and hid it beneath the floorboards. The crate was then transported to Goodfellow's engineering works on the outskirts of Stirling, where it was entrusted to Tommy Smith.

The smaller fragment of the Stone had an equally eventful journey. Indeed, this piece almost got no further than London's Knightsbridge. As the Anglia pulled away from traffic lights, the boot – which Hamilton had hurriedly closed as the policeman approached them at the abbey – sprang open and the Stone fell into the street outside Harrods department store. Fortunately, Matheson heard the thud and retrieved it from the road. She then made her way to friends in Birmingham, where the guest for Christmas lunch was the city's chief constable. Leaving the car and Stone in Birmingham, Matheson then made her way back to Scotland.

After returning to Glasgow, Hamilton later took the train to Birmingham to collect the Anglia and its contents. Late one night, some two weeks after receiving the Stone, Rollo was summoned to Bishopbriggs by David Forrester, secretary of the Covenant committee. There he was handed the smaller fragment of the Stone by Alan Stuart's father. Returning to Bonnybridge, Rollo hid it under his office desk before passing it to his co-director, James Scott, to conceal in his garage.

The taking of the Stone produced a wide range of reactions. Predictably, there was widespread outrage from the Establishment, which ignored the episode's political dimension. Addressing the nation, an agitated Dean of Westminster – Dr A.C. Don, a Scot – described the Stone's removal as an act of sacrilege. Dragging the king into the controversy, Don claimed that George VI – who had been informed of the Stone's 'theft' just before he gave his Christmas Day broadcast from Sandringham – was distressed about the incident. The Dean declared that he would go 'to the ends of the earth' to retrieve the Stone, although it was only in Kent as he spoke. Speaking in the House of Commons, the Home Secretary described the perpetrators as 'thieves and vulgar vandals', conveniently overlooking how the Stone had been obtained in the first place.

The reactions of 'fringe' religious groups were even more colourful. *Brith* pronounced that 'those who stole the Stone [had] lifted their hands against the Lord and against His anointed, and they, and all those who plotted and planned with them, are now cursed, and will suffer for the terrible crime they have committed'. Others speculated that the Stone's 'theft' was a omen signalling the end of the British monarchy.

Like the Stone itself, Scottish opinion was split. Many Scots rejoiced at the audacious cheek of the Stone's removal from Westminster Abbey and the incompetence of the police at apprehending the culprits and recovering the Stone. Others disapproved of the students' actions, but still believed that the Stone rightly belonged to Scotland and the Scots; the principle was right, even if the means were flawed. In contrast, Scottish church and political leaders were less enthusiastic and, eager to demonstrate or reinforce their respectability, variously criticised those responsible and/or appealed for the Stone to be handed over to the authorities. In particular, there was disquiet that George VI, who had recently led Britain through the Second World War, had become embroiled in the matter. But, overall, the Stone's removal was a cause for celebration by Scots and rejuvenated Scottish national consciousness.

67 *Crowds look on as police drag the Serpentine in London's Hyde Park looking for the Stone, 29 December 1950*

While the Stone was moved clandestinely around central Scotland, intense media speculation and extensive police enquiries continued. At first the police floundered around, clutching at straws. They dragged the Serpentine in London's Hyde Park following a tip-off that two men had pushed a stone off the bridge at Kensington Gardens (**67**). All cargo ships leaving London for Scottish ports were checked. The police searched the Highlands, paying close attention to known Scottish nationalist activists, including Wendy Wood, all of whom knew nothing of the Stone's whereabouts. Press speculation was rife, predicting that arrests were imminent and continually talking-up the prospects of an early conclusion to the case. A reward of £2,000, a substantial sum in 1951, was offered for information leading to the Stone's return and the conviction of the culprits. There were no takers.

Then the police developed some good leads. Glasgow's Mitchell Library had three books on the Stone and only two people had consulted them recently. One was an African, the other was Hamilton, who had requested all three books in November 1950, the month before the 'theft'. Police enquiries were now focused on Glasgow University and surveillance of Hamilton soon led them to Matheson. Separately, the police followed up a statement by an abbey attendant who had spoken to two Scotsmen the day before the Stone was taken and who told him they were from 'somewhere with a name like Forgen'. The police checked the addresses of each of the university's 7,000 students and came up with one name; Vernon was from Forgandenny, Perthshire. The noose was tightening.

But despite identifying and questioning the suspects, the police were no nearer locating the Stone, the location of which was by now unknown to the Stone-snatchers. And the students had no intention of admitting their role in the affair. In desperation, the police consulted a clairvoyant.

Despite a massive police investigation, the weeks passed and still there was no sign of the Stone. The group faced an unexpected dilemma: what to do with the Stone? They made the reasonable though naïve offer to 'return the Stone to the safe keeping of His Majesty's officers if he would graciously assure them that in all time coming the Stone will remain in Scotland'. Those holding the Stone believed that they had received such an assurance.

At the request of MacCormick and Gray, Rollo delivered the Stone, on a specially constructed mason's handbarrow, to Willie White in Bearsden on Easter Monday 1951. At White's house, Gray reunited the fragments with two brass rods and some cement. The Stone was then taken to Arbroath Abbey where it was left before the high altar. The location was a symbolic one, where the *Declaration of Arbroath* was signed in 1320. The Stone, still on its handbarrow and draped with a Saltire – the Cross of St Andrew, Scotland's national flag – was found there by James Wishart, the abbey custodian on 11 April 1951 (**68-70**).

Like its removal from Westminster Abbey, the Stone's abandonment to the authorities produced a range of reactions. Many Scots were mystified that the Stone, which had taken so long to recover, had been given up so easily and for no obvious benefit, especially when the police were no nearer recovering it. But those who took the Stone believed that they had made their point. Besides, they claimed, the Stone was of no use in hiding and, as it could not remain undetected indefinitely, it was better to return the Stone voluntarily

68 The Stone of Destiny, still on its handbarrow, as found at Arbroath Abbey on 11 April 1951. James Wishart, the Abbey custodian, holds the Saltire (Cross of St Andrew) which covered the Stone when it was found. Such was the interest in his discovery that Wishart had to cancel his day off the next day

69 *Senior policemen, having located their quarry at last, gather with onlookers around the newly-rediscovered Stone of Destiny at Arbroath Abbey, 11 April 1951*

than for it to be seized and those responsible arrested. But many Scots concluded that an opportunity to wring some political concessions from the Establishment had been lost.

No criminal charges were ever brought against those responsible for taking or concealing the Stone. These events have been portrayed in the 2008 film, *Stone of Destiny*.

THE DEBATE CONTINUES: 1951–96

From Arbroath, the Stone of Destiny was taken to Forfar police station and from there to Glasgow central police station. The Stone was then transported to London in the boot of a police car, to the indignation of many Scots who believed that such a revered object should have been treated with greater respect.

But the Stone's discovery and return to London were not the end of the matter. The Stone was not replaced in the Coronation Chair in Westminster Abbey for almost a year, but was instead kept in the Islip Chapel. While the Dean and Chapter feared another attempt to remove the Stone, the government re-examined the issue of where it should be kept. Such was its sensitivity that even the existence of this debate was kept secret until the 1990s. In 1951, the Secretary of State for Scotland, Hector McNeil, recommended to his Cabinet colleagues that the Stone should be restored to Scotland. But his fellow ministers, including the Prime Minister, Clement Attlee, remained unconvinced. And before the matter could be resolved, the Labour Party lost the 1951 general election. The incoming Conservative government, under Sir Winston Churchill, had no interest in upsetting the *status quo* by returning the Stone to Scotland. This decision was influenced by another factor. George VI was now seriously ill; before long, the Stone would have to play its historic role in the coronation of a British monarch once again.

The Stone was replaced beneath the seat of the Coronation Chair, without ceremony or publicity, on 26 February 1952. Later that day, and with the prior agreement of the leader of the opposition, Churchill announced to the House of Commons:

> For over 650 years the Stone has been in Westminster Abbey and, from its use at successive Coronations it has a historic significance for all the countries in the Commonwealth. With the approval of Her Majesty's Government, the Stone has been restored to its traditional place.

The Stone's Scottish dimension was conveniently ignored. The authorities hoped that, by denying publicity to the Stone's return, the controversy would go away.

The Stone's illicit removal from Westminster Abbey in 1950–51 might appear to have resulted in no long term gains. But these events soon became engrained in Scottish national consciousness and left a lasting impression, a source of inspiration for a stateless nation. The Stone and its 'theft' became a *cause célèbre*. Johnny McEvoy celebrated the

70 *Police remove the Stone of Destiny, recovered with its Saltire, from Arbroath Abbey, 11 April 1951*

episode in song with *The Wee Magic Stane*. And, inspired by a combination of modern myths and these events, Nigel Tranter's *The Stone* (1958) told the fictional story of the race for the 'real' Stone, Edward I having removed a substitute. A group of Scots, concerned that the Stone would be taken to England as soon as it is discovered, beat a team of Oxford University archaeologists to the Stone and hid it from the authorities. The twin issues of the Stone's authenticity and ownership were now inextricably interlinked and the subject of continued debate.

More Scots than ever were now aware of Scotland's greatest symbol of national identity. It was only a matter of time before someone else would attempt to repatriate the Stone. But, as the nationalist cause waned during the 1950s and 1960s, so did interest in the Stone. Nevertheless, on 14 June 1967 a young Scot made an unsuccessful attempt to remove the Stone from Westminster Abbey. John Patrick O'Burn (25) 'sincerely believed that the Stone belonged to the people of Scotland', but found it too heavy to lift. O'Burn was convicted at Bow Street Magistrates Court, fined £7 10s and placed on probation.

With the nationalist resurgence of the 1970s, passions concerning the Stone were again rekindled. The discovery of North Sea oil in the early 1970s gave many Scots a renewed sense of nationhood and allayed deeply-rooted fears that the Scottish economy could not survive independently from that of the UK. In the 1974 general elections, the SNP won seven seats in February, increasing this to 11 in October. Like a barometer of nationalist climate, interest in the Stone rose again.

On 4 September 1974, David Stewart (24), born in England of Scottish parents, made a single-handed bid to take the Stone. After reconnoitring the abbey the previous month, Stewart planned to remove the Stone from the Coronation Chair using a pulley, lower it onto a home-made trolley, remove it from the abbey using a ramp, and load it into his Mini. But security around Westminster was tight following an IRA bomb attack on the Houses of Parliament. And, on entering the abbey with most of his equipment, Stewart realised that he had forgotten his tools and only just made it back before closing time. Successfully hiding himself in the abbey, Stewart tried to remove the Stone from the Chair. But, like previous activists, he underestimated the Stone's weight. A cast iron finial on the railings surrounding the Coronation Chair, to which a rope was attached, broke under the strain. The Stone fell onto Stewart's trolley, causing it to collapse. An alarm linked to the Chair was activated and Stewart was arrested at the scene. Stewart was charged with theft and held on remand in Brixton Prison before charges were dropped and he was released.

Stewart claimed that his objective was to contest the issue of the Stone's ownership and that the most effective and high profile way of doing this was to be charged with theft. In bringing the case to court, the authorities would have to establish the ownership of the Stone. This they were clearly unwilling or unable to do.

The argument for Scottish devolution faltered in the late 1970s. In the referendum for a Scottish assembly in March 1979, 51.6% voted in favour but, on a relatively low turnout, fell below the 40% of the electorate required. And with the election of a Conservative government three months later, hopes of Scottish self-government were dashed once more. Interest in the Stone declined, although the issue resurfaced in 1984. That year, a House of Commons motion again called, unsuccessfully, for the Stone's return to Scotland and the UNESCO Cultural Committee rejected an application by the Scotland-

United Nations Group for the Stone's return on the grounds that it could not intervene in a domestic UK issue.

Not until the 1990s did the debate concerning the Stone resurface. Another generation was reminded of the events of 1950–51 by a new edition of Ian Hamilton's *The Taking of the Stone of Destiny* (1991). This was soon followed by Pat Gerber's *The Search for the Stone of Destiny* (1992). Paradoxically, Gerber claimed that the Stone then in Westminster Abbey was a fake or substitute, but also pressed for its return to Scotland. Faced with official inflexibility over the Stone's return to Scotland, many Scots appeared to be in denial. Rather than campaign for the Stone's return, they denied its authenticity with increasingly fanciful theories. But Gerber successfully raised the profile of the debate concerning the Stone's repatriation, receiving the endorsement of several influential Scots.

Robbie the Pict adopted a different approach, tirelessly pursuing the issue of the Stone's ownership through 'official channels'. In November 1993, Robbie attempted to report the Stone's theft, by Edward I in 1296, to the police. When they declined to pursue the case he contacted the Procurator Fiscal in Perth, the Lord Advocate in Edinburgh, the Scottish Office, the Scottish Secretary, the Home Secretary, the Prime Minister, the Dean of Westminster and, ultimately, the Queen herself. Although seemingly eccentric, Robbie's approach was legalistic. He pointed out that under Scots law there is no statute of limitations for the offences of theft or reset (handling stolen goods) and that the receiver can never acquire lawful title to stolen property. Therefore both the Queen and the Dean of Westminster, claimed Robbie, could be charged with reset. Not surprisingly, the authorities had no intention of pursuing the matter. The Stone, the Scottish Office claimed, was a 'royal peculiar', belonging to the Crown and in the custody of the Dean of Westminster. Undeterred by official obfuscation, Robbie continued writing, relentlessly pursuing legal, constitutional and logical inconsistencies in the replies he received.

Robbie also requested the Stone's return, initially to Letham in Angus, and set the Queen a deadline of midnight on 19 May 1995, the eve of the 1310th anniversary of the Battle of Nechtansmere, in which the Picts defeated an invading Northumbrian army. By March 1996, Robbie was campaigning against high tolls on the newly opened bridge linking the Isle of Skye with the mainland. The Sketis Heritage Trust, of which Robbie was spokesman, was formed specifically to bring the Stone to Skye as a tourist attraction. The Trust offered £250,000 for the Stone but immediately encountered difficulties in identifying the Stone's owner. Another round of letter writing ensued.

THE STONE RESTORED: 1996

The Stone was firmly on the Scottish agenda by the mid-1990s. Robbie the Pict had helpfully informed both the Prime Minister and Scottish Secretary of the forthcoming 700th anniversary of the Stone's removal from Scotland and that the Stone's return would earn them a place in Scottish history. Political leaders began to take an interest: in 1995, Alex Salmond, the SNP leader, called for the Stone's return to Scotland. But, even so, there was little indication of the dramatic events to come.

On 3 July 1996, the then Prime Minister, John Major, made a brief statement to the House of Commons:

> The Stone of Destiny is the most ancient symbol of Scottish kingship. It was used in the coronation of Scottish Kings until the end of the 13th century. Exactly 700 years ago, in 1296, King Edward I brought it from Scotland and housed it in Westminster Abbey. The Stone remains the property of the Crown. I wish to inform the House that, on the advice of Her Majesty's Ministers, The Queen has agreed that the Stone should be returned to Scotland. The Stone will, of course, be taken to Westminster Abbey to play its traditional role in the coronation ceremonies of future sovereigns of the United Kingdom.
>
> The Stone of Destiny holds a special place in the hearts of Scots. On this, the 700th anniversary of its removal from Scotland, it is appropriate to return it to its historic homeland. I am sure that the House would wish to be assured that the Stone will be placed in an appropriate setting in Scotland. The Government will be consulting Scottish and Church opinion about that. The Stone might be displayed in Edinburgh Castle alongside the Honours of Scotland, Europe's oldest crown jewels. Alternatively, it might be appropriate to place it in St Margaret's Chapel inside the Castle or in St Giles' Cathedral. There may be other options.
>
> Once those consultations have been completed, the necessary arrangements will be made and the Stone will be installed with due dignity in Scotland.

Predictably, reactions to the announcement varied. Opposition leaders welcomed the decision, but Scottish Labour MPs reacted with cynical derision. There was much surprise, but little rejoicing in Scotland, where the Stone's return was viewed as a feeble substitute for genuine political action and constitutional reform. Indeed, there was anger and disbelief in some quarters that, at a time when most Scots wanted devolved government and more jobs, all they were being given was the Stone. The government's action was condemned as a patronising gesture, displaying a characteristic insensitivity to Scottish aspirations. Scotland's needs had moved on: the Scots wanted a better future, not a symbol of the past.

Some sections of the English press were equally hostile, but for different reasons. The London *Evening Standard* described the Stone's return as 'an act of indefensible vandalism', while the *Spectator* criticised John Major's 'facile and throwaway approach' and the 'monumental cheek of implicating the monarch in party political interest at the expense of our national monarchy'. Historian Paul Binski argued that the Stone was as much English as Scottish after 700 years in Westminster Abbey, 'a symbol of the Union governed from Westminster' and therefore ought to stay where it was. Shocked by the government's decision, the Dean and Chapter of Westminster Abbey issued a thinly-veiled warning:

> as the successors of those Abbots of Westminster and Deans and Chapters who have been guardians of the Stone for so many centuries, we must continue to urge those who are advising the Queen in this manner to take full account of the symbolic and

emotional significance of the Stone, its integral connection with the Coronation Chair which was made in 1301 to contain it, and its intimate association with the Sacrament of Coronation.

The Dean and Chapter believe that the Stone should not be regarded as a secular museum piece and that its religious associations should be considered most carefully and respected in whatever decisions are made about its future location.

Another controversy arose over the Stone's proposed setting in Scotland. Many sites were suggested, including the new National Museum of Scotland in Edinburgh, the proposed Scottish parliament and, of course, Scone. The Scottish Office published a consultation paper and invited comments on where the Stone might be housed and displayed. Of 113 responses received, 47 wanted the Stone to be kept in Edinburgh and, of these, 29 – only 25% of the total – favoured the Castle. Opinion polls showed that 56% of Scots preferred the Stone to be kept at its historic location of Scone. But the government decided that the Stone should be kept in the Crown Room at Edinburgh Castle alongside the Honours of Scotland, just as John Major had suggested on 3 July (**colour plate 27**). Scone was ruled unsuitable because it was privately owned and had no appropriate facilities.

The decision to display the Stone in the Crown Room was based on 'history, accessibility and security', Michael Forsyth, the Secretary of State for Scotland, announced. But the Stone has nothing to do with the Honours, which date from the sixteenth century and reflect a very different style of kingship. And the Stone's only historical association with Edinburgh Castle was that it was kept there temporarily on its way south after it was seized by Edward I. Moreover, the cramped conditions in which it is displayed, combined with the crowds it attracts, ensures that the Stone is not as accessible as it could or should be. But the Crown Room's security is undeniable and this appears to have been the paramount factor in selecting a location for the Stone. Although the debate continued after the Stone's installation and the election of a Labour government, the Scottish Secretary, by then the late Donald Dewar, announced in August 1997 that the Stone would remain in the Crown Room.

In a complex and lengthy operation, the Stone was removed from its resting place underneath the seat of the Coronation Chair on the evening of 13 November 1996. The Stone was then placed in a specially-built crated handbarrow and left to stand in the Abbey's Lantern overnight. The Stone was removed from Westminster Abbey by uniformed security guards under cover of darkness the next morning (**colour plate 10**). The Dean of Westminster, the Very Rev Michael Mann, spoke of feeling 'bereaved' by its loss. The Stone, in a police Land Rover and under army escort, was then taken north amid high security and intense secrecy. The authorities were determined not to lose the Stone on this occasion. The Stone was kept overnight under army guard in Albemarle Barracks, Northumbria, before continuing on its journey the next morning.

With an escort from the Coldstream Guards, the Stone crossed onto the bridge over the River Tweed at Coldstream. At the mid-point on the bridge, marking the Anglo-Scottish border, the Stone was received by the Scottish Secretary, representatives of

Scottish political parties and local dignitaries. At 11.05 am on 15 November, the Stone of Destiny was in Scotland once more. It was an hour and five minutes late, the result of a bomb scare, but after 700 years it scarcely mattered. Responsibility for the Stone's escort was handed over to the King's Own Scottish Borderers and a pipe band greeted it with a specially composed quick march, *The Return of the Stone*. But there was disappointment and suspicion amongst the small crowd that the Stone was not on display. Carried in a convoy of two army Land Rovers and a white minibus, it was widely felt that the pomp did not match the circumstance.

The Stone's official handing-over was intended to be a more ceremonial occasion, with a perspex-topped army Land Rover – the 'stone-mobile' – to display and protect the Stone. On 30 November 1996, St Andrew's Day, the Stone was escorted from Holyrood Palace, the Queen's official residence in Scotland, up the Royal Mile to St Giles' Cathedral. Soldiers in full ceremonial dress and fluttering Saltires lined the route. References to the Stone were incorporated in the service held there. The Moderator of the General Assembly of the Church of Scotland, the Right Rev John McIndoe, hailed the Stone's return as a 'substantial landmark':

> during all the long pilgrimage of the years, the ideal of Scottish nationhood and the reality of Scottish identity have never been wholly obliterated from the hearts of the people. The recovery of this ancient symbol of the Stone cannot but strengthen the proud distinctiveness of the people of Scotland. It will in addition bear a silent and steady witness to the mutuality of interest between those who govern and those who are governed, united in the task of promoting the welfare of the land and the destination of its people.

From St Giles', the Stone continued up the Royal Mile to Edinburgh Castle, where it was installed on a red-carpeted dais in the Great Hall. There, HRH the Duke of York, Prince Andrew, representing the Queen, formally handed the Stone over to the Scottish Secretary, in his capacity as Keeper of the Great Seal of Scotland and representing the Commissioners of the Regalia. Forsyth lost no opportunity in making a political point about Scotland's constitutional status:

> I will speak for the people of Scotland when I say how important the return of the Stone is to us. We are grateful to Her Majesty the Queen for graciously approving the return of the Stone to its ancient homeland, where it will continue to be a powerful reminder of Scotland's heritage and a symbol of our continuity as a nation within the United Kingdom.

A sense of unreality pervaded the days' proceedings, captured by the band of the Royal Marines which accompanied the Stone from Holyrood Palace with the *Mission Impossible* theme tune. There was no established protocol for such an occasion, so the Stone was given the same reception as a visiting head of state. Four Tornado jets screamed over the castle to mark its arrival. A 21-gun salute sounded from the castle esplanade after the handover and was returned by HMS *Newcastle*, moored in the Port of Leith.

But while tourists seemed excited by the spectacle, many Scots felt that something was missing. The crowds were smaller than anticipated and greeted the Stone in silence, unimpressed with the gesture of its return, the ceremony or the Stone itself. Freshly rehearsed doubts about the Stone's authenticity also contributed to the apathy. The occasion, with its patriotic symbolism, processions, military bands, armed guards and a host of officials in a variety of outlandish uniforms, exposed the British and Scottish Establishments at their most traditional and vulnerable. The organisers had misjudged the public mood.

The government appeared to believe it was making a serious and substantial concession to Scottish national sentiment. But the Stone's return did nothing to address Scottish aspirations, whether for national self-determination or greater social democracy. Even the London *Evening Standard* commented that 'Short of sending a consignment of beads to the natives, it is hard to imagine a more patronising and clumsy gesture by a Westminster government, designed to buy off the restless Scots'. The Stone was back in Scotland but there was still a sense of unfinished business.

A DESTINY FULFILLED?

The Stone of Destiny's return to Scotland in 1996 represents the most recent leg of its remarkable journeys in space and time. But the wider political context within which this occurred leads back to the start of this book and the prophecy associated with the Stone, and forward to Scotland's new political future.

The motives behind the government's initiative to return the Stone to Scotland attracted considerable debate. At Coldstream, Michael Forsyth had claimed: 'I learned about the Stone of Destiny when I was seven years old and I always believed that it should be in Scotland. There was no political agenda here at all. Its return is not going to make a huge difference, but it's an important part of our heritage'. But many Scots were sceptical, viewing the decision as politically motivated. After 17 years in power, why had it taken the Conservatives so long to return the Stone? Was it simply a coincidence that the Stone's return was announced only two days before John Major made his first appearance before the Scottish Grand Committee, comprising all 72 Scottish MPs, in Dumfries? And with a general election imminent, some claimed that the Stone was returned simply to enable Forsyth to portray himself as a defender of Scottish interests. It was, they claimed, a public relations stunt and a blatant attempt to boost the Conservative Party's flagging electoral prospects in Scotland. Political commentators and cartoonists had a field day (**71**). Although they had won the 1992 general election, the Conservatives took only eleven Scottish seats. And their support sunk further. In the 1995 elections for Scotland's newly created single-tier local authorities, the Conservatives received only 11% of the total vote and gained control of no councils. The Conservatives needed all the help they could get, their critics claimed.

But if electoral dividends were the motivation, the Stone's return had little effect and may even have been counter-productive. The Conservatives not only lost the May 1997 general election but also failed to win a single Scottish seat. Michael Forsyth was knighted after losing his seat and incorporated the Stone in his coat of arms, prompting claims that it had been stolen once again.

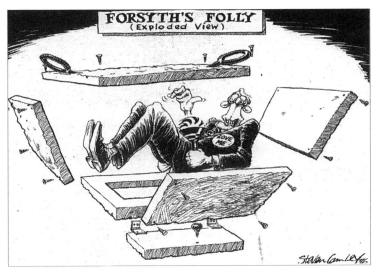

73 *A cartoon satirising Michael Forsyth's attempt to ingratiate John Major to the Scottish electorate by returning the Stone of Destiny to Scotland.* Steven Camley, *Scotland on Sunday,* November 1996

On the day of the Stone's installation in Edinburgh Castle, leaders of the Scottish Constitutional Convention issued the Declaration of Edinburgh, demanding a devolved assembly for Scotland. Canon Kenyon Wright, the convention's executive committee chairman, read the declaration before Edinburgh's Royal High School, the building converted to house a Scottish Assembly before the 1979 referendum:

> Today, Scotland's Stone of Destiny is returned, with elaborate ceremonial. We welcome the Stone, as a historic symbol of our nation's understanding of power and the conviction that sovereignty comes from the people. Scotland's true destiny, however, lies not in the past but in the future ... We say Yes to Scotland's true Destiny. We say Yes to Scotland's Parliament, which is Scotland's right.

The creation of a Scottish Parliament was one of the top priorities for the incoming Labour government. In the referendum of September 1997, 74.3% of the electorate voted for a Scottish Parliament, with 63.5% in favour of it having tax-raising powers. The long battle for Scottish devolution had at last been won, and won convincingly. The first elections to the Scottish Parliament were held in May 1999, assuming the powers formerly held by the Scottish Secretary and exercised through the Scottish Office. For the first time since 1707, Scotland had regained its own parliament and Scots the right to determine their own affairs.

Has the Destiny of the Stone been fulfilled at last? It is impossible not to be reminded of the ancient prophecy associated with the Stone, that wherever the Stone is placed, the Scots shall rule. The Stone was returned to Scotland only months before the referendum on a Scottish Parliament, but was there any link between the two events? Despite the range of reactions prompted by the Stone's return, it focused attention not just on Scotland's past but also on Scotland's current and future national identity and constitutional status. As a result, the Stone's restoration stimulated the debate and probably assisted the argument in favour of devolution. Perhaps, as the age-old prophecy maintains, the Stone of Destiny and Scottish fortunes are inextricably interlinked.

SELECT BIBLIOGRAPHY

Barrow, G.W.S. 1997. Observations on the Coronation Stone of Scotland. *Scottish Historical Review* **76**: 115-21.

Breeze, D., Clancy, T. and Welander R. (eds) forthcoming. *The Stone of Destiny*. Edinburgh.

Breeze, D. and G. Munro 1997. *The Stone of Destiny: Symbol of Nationhood*. Edinburgh.

Elibank, Lord 1952. *The Coronation Stone*. London.

Gerber, P. 1992. *The Search for the Stone of Destiny*. Edinburgh. New ed. published 1997 as *Stone of Destiny*.

Hilton, J. 1897. *The Coronation Stone at Westminster Abbey*. Reprinted from the *Archaeological Journal*. London.

Hunter, J. 1856. King Edward's spoliations in Scotland in AD 1296 – the Coronation Stone – original and unpublished evidence. *Archaeological Journal* **13**: 245-55.

Legge, M.D. (trans.) 1959. La Piere d'Escoce. *Scottish Historical Review* **38**: 109-13.

McAuslane, M. 1988. The Stone of Destiny. *The Sunday Mail Story of Scotland* **1**.4: 108-12.

Nimmo, J.M. 1996. The Stone of Destiny. *Scottish Genealogist* **42** (1995): 49-54.

Robertson, J. 1868. The Coronation Stone. (Letter dated 7 July 1866). In Stanley 1868: 492-99.

Rutherford, A. 1937. *The Coronation Chair and the Stone of Destiny*. London.

Simpson, W.D. 1958. *Dunstaffnage Castle and the Stone of Destiny*. Edinburgh.

Skene, W.F. 1869. *The Coronation Stone*. Edinburgh. Also published in *Proceedings of the Society of Antiquaries of Scotland* **8** (1868–70): 68-99.

Stanley, A.P. 1868. *Historical Memorials of Westminster Abbey*. London.

Stuart, J. 1870. Note on the Coronation Stone. *Proceedings of the Society of Antiquaries of Scotland* **8** (1868–70): 99-105.

Toland, J. 1709. *A Critical History of the Celtic Religion and Learning*. London.

Watson, G. 1910. The Coronation Stone of Scotland. *Transactions of the Scottish Ecclesiological Society* **3**.1 (1909–10): 13-31

Welander, R., Breeze, D.J. and Clancy, T.O. (eds) 2003. *The Stone of Destiny: Artefact and Icon,* Society of Antiquaries of Scotland Monograph Series 22, Edinburgh.

1 The name and prophecy of the Stone

Ó Broin, T. 1990. Lia Fáil: fact and fiction in the tradition. *Celtica* **21**: 393-401.

O'Reilly, P.J. 1902. Notes on the coronation stone at Westminster, and the *Lia Fáil* at Tara. *Journal of the Royal Society of Antiquaries of Scotland* **32**: 77-92.

O'Rourke, J. 1881. The Lia Fail, or Stone of Destiny. *Irish Ecclesiastical Record* **1** (1880) (3rd series): 440-53.

Petrie, G. 1838. On the history and antiquities of Tara Hill. *Transactions of the Royal Irish Academy* **53** (1832–38): 25-232.

Ua Clerigh, A. n.d. [c.1907]. The Lia Fail - the Stone of Destiny. In A. Ua Clerigh, *The History of Ireland to the Coming of Henry II*, 246-56. London.

2 Mythical origins

The evolution of the myth

Broun, D. 1997. The birth of Scottish history. *Scottish Historical Review* **76**: 4-22.

Broun, D. 1999. *The Irish Identity of the Kingdom of the Scots*. Studies in Celtic History 18. Woodbridge.

The origins of the myth

MacEoin, G.S. 1964. On the Irish legend of the origins of the Picts. *Studia Hibernica* **4**: 164.

Carey, J. 1993. *A New Introduction ... to Lebor Gabála Érenn = the Book of the Taking of Ireland*. London.

Scowcroft, R.M. 1987. Leabhar Gabhála - Part I: the growth of the text. *Ériu* **38**: 81-142.

Scowcroft, R.M. 1988. Leabhar Gabhála - Part II: the growth of the tradition. *Ériu* **39**: 1-66.

Myths in action

The abstracts from English chronicles made at Edward's command are edited in:

Palgrave, F. 1837. *Documents and Records Illustrating the History of Scotland*, pp 56-137. London.

Cowan, E.J. 1984. Myth and identity in early medieval Scotland. *Scottish Historical Review* **63**: 111-35.

Goldstein, R.J. 1991. The Scottish mission to Boniface VIII in 1301: a reconsideration of the context of the *Instructiones* and *Processus*. *Scottish Historical Review* **70**: 1-15.

Matthews, W. 1970. The Egyptians in Scotland: the political history of a myth. *Viator: Medieval and Renaissance Studies* **1**: 289-306.

Stones, E.L.G. (ed. & trans.) 1965. *Anglo-Scottish Relations, 1174-1328: Some Selected Documents*. Second ed. 1970. Oxford.

Stones, E.L.G. 1969. The appeal to history in Anglo-Scottish relations between 1291 and 1401. *Archives: Journal of the British Records Association* **9**: 11-21, 80-83.

3 The Stone
Physical appearance
Hill, P. 2003. 'The Stone of Destiny examined: an overview and discussion', in Welander *et al.* (eds) 2003: 11–31.
Geology
Barnett, J.B. 1872. Jacob's Stone. *Jewish Chronicle*, 11 October 1872, pp 380-81.
Davidson, C.F. 1938. The geology of the Coronation Stone. *Transactions of the Perthshire Society of Natural Science* **9.7**: 210-13.
Davidson, C.F. 1951. The Stone of Destiny. *The Illustrated London News*, 13 January 1951, pp 20-21.
Fortey, N.J., E.R. Phillips, A.A. McMillan and M.A.E. Browne 1998. A geological perspective on the Stone of Destiny. *Scottish Journal of Geology* **34.2**: 145-52.
Geikie, A. 1869. Letter dated 23 April 1869. In Skene 1869: 50.
Geikie, A. 1895. *Memoir of Sir Andrew Crombie Ramsay*. London.
Haes, F. 1872. Jacob's Stone. *Jewish Chronicle*, 6 September 1872, p. 311.
MacCulloch, J. 1819. *A Description of the Western Islands of Scotland*. 2 vols. London.
MacCulloch, J. 1824. *The Highlands and Western Isles of Scotland*. 4 vols. London.
Phillips, E., McMillan, A., Browne, M. and Fortey, N. 2003. 'The geology of the Stone of Destiny', in Welander *et al.* (eds) 2003: 33-40.
Pococke, R. 1887. *Tours in Scotland, 1747, 1750, 1760*. Ed. D.W. Kemp. Edinburgh.
Ramsay, A.C. 1868. Geological account of the Coronation Stone. In Stanley 1868: 499-501.
Possible earlier functions
Christie, J.B.T. 1970. Doubts about 'the Stone'. *The Scots Magazine* **94** (November 1970): 144-52.
Clapham, A.W. 1942. Anniversary address. *Antiquaries Journal* **22**: 157-66.

4 The authenticity of the Stone
'Antiquarius' 1781. *Gentleman's Magazine* **51** (1781): 452-53; **52** (1782): 22-23.
Ascherson, N. 2003. 'Significance of the Stone', in Welander *et al.* (eds) 2003: 261-33 .
Breeze, D.J. 2003. 'The Stone of Destiny: its origin, history and authenticity', in Welander *et al.* (eds) 2003: 3-8.
Heyde, D.E. 1954. The Stone of Destiny: is it in Scotland? *The Scots Magazine* **61** (May 1954): 166, 168.
Hutcheson, A. 1927. The Scottish Coronation Stone: is it at Westminster? In A. Hutcheson, *Old Stories in Stones and Other Stories*, 199-219. Dundee.
McKerracher, A.C. 1984. Where is the real stone? *The Scots Magazine* **122** (December 1984): 271-79
'Special correspondents' 1975. The destiny of the Stone? *The Scots Magazine* **104** (November 1975): 201.
Medieval depictions
Birch, W. de Gray 1907. *History of Scottish Seals*. 2 vols. Stirling.
Richardson, J.S. 1951. The 'Stone of Destiny': early Scottish enthronements. *The Scotsman*, 17 February 1951.
The 'Dunsinane Stone'
Aitchison, N. 1999. *Macbeth: Man and Myth*. Stroud.

5 The Stone at Scone
Royal Commission on the Ancient and Historical Monuments of Scotland 1994. *South-East Perth: an Archaeological Landscape*. n.p. [Edinburgh].
Early medieval Scone
Alcock, L. 1982. Forteviot: a Pictish and Scottish royal church and palace. In S.M. Pearce (ed.), *The Early Church in Western Britain and Ireland: Studies Presented to C.A. Ralegh Radford*, 211-39. BAR British Series 102. Oxford.
Alcock, L. and E.A. Alcock 1992. Reconnaissance excavations on early historic fortifications and other royal sites in Scotland, 1974–1984; 5: A. Excavations & other fieldwork at Forteviot, Perthshire, 1981.... *Proceedings of the Society of Antiquaries of Scotland* **122**: 215-87.
Campbell, J. 1979. Bede's words for places. In P.H. Sawyer (ed.), *Names, Words and Graves: Early Medieval Settlement*, 34-54. Leeds.
Driscoll, S.T. 1991. The archaeology of state formation in Scotland. In W.S. Hanson and E.A. Slater (eds), *Scottish Archaeology: New Perceptions*, 81-111. Aberdeen.
Driscoll, S.T. 1998. Picts and prehistory: cultural resource management in early medieval Scotland. *World Archaeology* **30**: 142-58.
Driscoll, S.T. 1998. Political discourse and the growth of Christian ceremonialism in Pictland: the place of the St Andrews sarcophagus. In S.M. Foster (ed.), *The St Andrews Sarcophagus: a Pictish Masterpiece and its International Connections*, 168-78. Dublin.
Driscoll, S.T. 2004. 'The archaeological context of assembly in early medieval Scotland – Scone and its comparanda', in A. Pantos and S. Semple (eds), *Assembly Places and Practices in Medieval Europe*, 73-94.
Woolf, A. 2006. 'Dun Nechtain, Fortriu and the geography of the Picts', *Scottish Historical Review* **85** (2): 182-201.

Scone Abbey

Liber Ecclesie de Scon: *Liber Ecclesie de Scon: munimenta vetustiora Monasterii Sancte Trinitatis et Sancti Michaelis de Scon*. Bannatyne Club 78. Edinburgh (1843).

Clancy, T.O. 1995. '*Annat* in Scotland and the origins of the parish', *Innes Review* **46**: 91-115.

Duncan, A.M.M. 1966. The early parliaments of Scotland. *Scottish Historical Review* **45**: 36- 58.

Fawcett, R. 2003. 'The buildings of Scone Abbey', in Welander *et al.* (eds) 2003: 169-80.

MacDonald, A. 1973. 'Annat' in Scotland: a provisional review. *Scottish Studies* **17**: 135-46.

The inaugurations of Alexander III and John Balliol

Bannerman, J. 1989. The king's poet and the inauguration of Alexander III. *Scottish Historical Review* **68**: 120-49.

Broun, D. 2003. 'The origin of the Stone of Scone as a national icon', in Welander *et al.* (eds) 2003: 183-97.

Duncan, A.A.M. 2003. 'Before coronation: making a king at Scone in the 13th Century', in Welander *et al.* (eds) 2003: 139-67

Dumville, D.N. 1977. Kingship, genealogies and regnal lists. In Sawyer and Wood (eds) 1977: 72-104.

Legge, M.D. 1946. The inauguration of Alexander III. *Proceedings of the Society of Antiquaries of Scotland* **80** (1945–46): 73-82.

Scott, W.W. 1971. Fordun's description of the inauguration of Alexander II. *Scottish Historical Review* **50**: 198-200.

Stones, thrones and mounds

Adkins, R.A. and M.R. Petchey 1985. Secklow Hundred mound and other meeting place mounds in England. *Archaeological Journal* **141** (1984): 243-51.

Airlie, S. 2003. 'Thrones, dominions, powers: some European points of comparison for the Stone of Destiny', in Welander *et al.* (eds) 2003: 123-36.

Barrow, G.W.S. 1992. Popular courts. In G.W.S. Barrow, *Scotland and its Neighbours in the Middle Ages*, 217-46. London. First published as: Popular courts in early medieval Scotland: some suggested place-name evidence. *Scottish Studies* **25** (1981): 1-24.

Brash, R. Rolt 1865. On ancient stone chairs and stones of inauguration. *Gentleman's Magazine and Historical Review* **18**: 429-36, 548-58.

Caldwell, D.H. 2003. 'Finlaggan, Islay – stones and inauguration ceremonies', in Welander *et al.* (eds) 2003: 61-75.

Campbell, E. 2003. 'Royal inaugurations in Dal Riata and the Stone of Destiny', in Welander *et al.* (eds) 2003: 43-59.

Clancy, T.O. 2003. 'King-making and images of kingship in medieval Gaelic literature', in Welander *et al.* (eds) 2003: 85-105.

Cross, H. 1956. The Kingston Coronation Stone and the Coronations at Kingston-upon-Thames. Unpublished typescript in British Library.

Dillon, M. 1961. The inauguration of O'Conor. In J.A. Watt, J.B. Morrall and F.X. Martin (eds), *Medieval Studies Presented to Aubrey Gwynn*, 186-202. Dublin.

FitzPatrick, E. 2003. '*Leaca* and Gaelic inauguration ritual in medieval Ireland', in Welander *et al.* (eds) 2003: 107-21.

Frazer, Dr 1898. The Clandeboy O'Neills' stone inauguration chair. *Journal of the Royal Society of Antiquaries of Ireland* **28**: 254-7.

Hartland, E.S. 1903. The voice of the Stone of Destiny: an enquiry into the choice of kings by augury. *Folk-Lore* **14**: 28-60.

Hayes-McCoy, G.A. 1970. The making of an O'Neill: a view of the ceremony at Tullaghoge, Co. Tyrone. *Ulster Journal of Archaeology* **33**: 89-94

Hore, H.F. 1857. Inauguration of Irish chiefs. *Ulster Journal of Archaeology* **5**: 216-35.

Herity, M. 1995. Motes and mounds at royal sites in Ireland. *Journal of the Royal Society of Antiquaries of Ireland* **123** (1993): 127-51.

O'Donovan, J. 1844. Inauguration of Irish chiefs. In J. O'Donovan (ed. and trans.), *The Genealogies, Tribes, and Customs of Hy-Fiachrach*, 425-52. Dublin.

Thomas, F.W.L. 1879. Dunadd, Glassary, Argyllshire; the place of inauguration of the Dalriadic kings. *Proceedings of the Society of Antiquaries of Scotland* **13** (1878–79): 28-47.

Scone after the Stone

Coronation at Scone: *The Forme and Order of the Coronation [of Charles I] at Scoone, the first day of January, 1651*. Aberdeen (1651). Reprinted Paisley (1821).

Cooper, J. 1902. *Four Scottish Coronations. (The Coronations of James VI, Anne, Queen of James VI, Charles I, Charles II)*. Aberdeen.

Walker, D. 1970. Scone Palace, Perthshire. In H. Colvin and J. Harris (eds), *The Country Seat*, 210-14. London.

Stuart, J.P.C. (Marquess of Bute) 1902. *Scottish Coronations*. London.

6 The Stone at Westminster

Edward I and the Stone

Binski, P. 1995. *Westminster Abbey and the Plantagenets: Kingship and the Representation of Power 1200–1400*. New Haven.

Burges, W. 1863. The Coronation Chair. In G.G. Scott, *Gleanings from Westminster Abbey*, 121-26. Oxford.

Hallam, E. 1974–77. *Itinerary of Edward I*. 3 vols. List and Index Society 103, 132, 135.

Stones, E.L.G. and G.G. Simpson (eds) 1978. *Edward I and the Throne of Scotland, 1290- 1296*. 2 vols. Oxford.

Prestwich, M. 1997. *Edward I*. Second ed. First published 1988. New Haven.

Watson, F. 1998. *Under the Hammer: Edward I and Scotland, 1286–1307*. East Linton.

English myths

Acklom, S. 1915. *The British Coronation Stone: its Practical and Spiritual Relationship to the British Race. The Testimony of Scripture*. London.

Allen, J.H. 1902. *Judah's Sceptre and Joseph's Birthright*. London.

Barnett, J.B. 1872. Jacob's Stone. *Jewish Chronicle*, 13 September 1872, pp 323-24.

Bowser, S.F. 1932. *The Bowser Card of the Jacob Stone*. Fort Wayne, Indiana.

Connon, F.W. 1951. *The Stone of Destiny, or the Stone that Binds a Commonwealth*. London.

Fowler, C. 1951. *The Amazing History of the Stone of Destiny*. London.

Rogers, G.A. 1881. *The Coronation Stone; and England's Interest in it*. London.

Rogers, E.M. 1902. *The Witnessing Stone in Westminster Abbey. The Coronation of King Edward VII*. Third ed. London.

Shaw, E.M. 1925. *How the Coronation Stone came to Westminster*. London.

The Coronation Stone

Binski, P. 2003. 'A "sign of victory": the Coronation Chair, its manufacture, setting and symbolism', in Welander *et al.* (eds) 2003: 207-22.

Hillam, D. 2001. *Crown, Orb and Sceptre: the True Stories of English Coronations*. Stroud.

H.F. (née F) 1854. *Notes and Queries*, 8 April 1854.

Jones, W. 1883. *Crowns and Coronations: A History of Regalia*. London.

Legg, L.G.W. 1902. *Suggestions for the Reconstruction of the Coronation Ceremonies*. Church Historical Society Publications 67. London.

Murray, R.H. 1936. *The King's Crowning*. London.

Palmer, W. 1953. *The Coronation Chair*. London.

Perkins, J.H.T. 1902. *The Coronation Book; or, the Hallowing of the Sovereigns of England*. London. Second ed. 1911.

Perkins, J. 1937. *The Crowning of the Sovereign of Great Britain and the Dominions Overseas: a Handbook to the Coronation*. London. Second ed. 1953.

Ratcliff, E.C. 1953. *The Coronation Service of Her Majesty Queen Elizabeth II*. Cambridge.

Richardson, H.G. 1938. Early coronation records. *Bulletin of the Institute of Historical Research* **16**: 1-11.

Richardson, H.G. 1960. The coronation in medieval England. *Traditio* **16**: 111-202.

Schramm, P.E. 1937. *A History of the English Coronation*. Trans. L.G.W. Legg. Oxford.

Stacpoole, W.H. 1911. *The Coronation Regalia: an Excursion into a Curious Bypath of Literature*. First published 1902. London.

Royal Commission on Historical Monuments (England) 1924. *An Inventory of the Historical Monuments in London, vol. 1: Westminster Abbey*. London

The Stone in English literature

Rye, W.B. 1865. *England as Seen by Foreigners in the Days of Elizabeth and James the First*. London.

7 The Stone returns

Early attempts

Barrow, G.W.S. 2003. 'The removal of the Stone and attempts at recovery, to 1328', in Welander *et al.* (eds) 2003: 199-205.

Stones, E.L.G. 1949. The English mission to Edinburgh in 1328. *Scottish Historical Review* **28**: 121-32.

Stones, E.L.G. 1950. An addition to the 'Rotuli Scotiae'. *Scottish Historical Review* **29**: 23- 51.

Stones, E.L.G. 1953. The Treaty of Northampton. *History* **28**: 54-61.

The Stone retrieved: 1950-51

Anon. 1951. The stolen Stone. *'Brith': Britain Know Thyself* **62** (January 1951): 8-17.

Hamilton, I.R. 1952. *No Stone Unturned*. London.

Hamilton, I. 1988. Bringing it home. *The Sunday Mail Story of Scotland* **1.4**: 85-87.

Hamilton, I.R. 1990. *A Touch of Treason*. Moffat.

Hamilton, I.R. 1991. *The Taking of the Stone of Destiny*. Moffat.

McBeth, J. 1997. Stone of Scone: archives reveal how stone-snatchers were caught. *Avenue: the Magazine for Graduates and Friends of the University of Glasgow* **21** (January 1997): 15- 16.

Munro, G. 2003. 'The Stone of Destiny in modern times', in Welander *et al.* (eds) 2003: 225-33.

The Stone restored: 1996

Binski, P. 1996. Even more English than Scottish. *Spectator* 13 July 1996, 11-13.

Burnett, C.J. and C.J. Tabraham 1993. *The Honours of Scotland: the Story of the Scottish Crown Jewels*. Edinburgh.

Ritchie, J. and R. Brydon 1996. Shadow of a dream. *Chapman* **85**: 6-11.

Welander, R. 2003. 'The events of 1996', in Welander *et al.* (eds) 2003: 235-59.

INDEX